Computer users are not all alike.
Neither are SYBEX books.

We know our customers have a variety of needs. They've told us so. And because we've listened, we've developed several distinct types of books to meet the needs of each of our customers. What are you looking for in computer help?

If you're looking for the basics, try the **ABC's** series. You'll find short, unintimidating tutorials and helpful illustrations. For a more visual approach, select **Teach Yourself**, featuring screen-by-screen illustrations of how to use your latest software purchase.

Mastering and **Understanding** titles offer you a step-by-step introduction, plus an in-depth examination of intermediate-level features, to use as you progress.

Our **Up & Running** series is designed for computer-literate consumers who want a no-nonsense overview of new programs. Just 20 basic lessons, and you're on your way.

We also publish two types of reference books. Our **Instant References** provide quick access to each of a program's commands and functions. SYBEX **Encyclopedias** provide a *comprehensive reference* and explanation of all of the commands, features and functions of the subject software.

Sometimes a subject requires a special treatment that our standard series doesn't provide. So you'll find we have titles like **Advanced Techniques, Handbooks, Tips & Tricks**, and others that are specifically tailored to satisfy a unique need.

We carefully select our authors for their in-depth understanding of the software they're writing about, as well as their ability to write clearly and communicate effectively. Each manuscript is thoroughly reviewed by our technical staff to ensure its complete accuracy. Our production department makes sure it's easy to use. All of this adds up to the highest quality books available, consistently appearing on best seller charts worldwide.

You'll find SYBEX publishes a variety of books on every popular software package. Looking for computer help? Help Yourself to SYBEX.

For a complete catalog of our publications:

SYBEX Inc.
2021 Challenger Drive, Alameda, CA 94501
Tel: (415) 523-8233/(800) 227-2346 Telex: 336311
SYBEX Fax: (415) 523-2373

Up & Running with Quicken® 4

Darleen Hartley Yourzek

SYBEX®

San Francisco • Paris • Düsseldorf • Soest

To Brenda Barlow, a dear friend who was always concise and to the point, just like this book. We miss you.

Acquisitions Editor: Dianne King
Series Editor: Joanne Cuthbertson
Editor: Marilyn Smith
Project Editor: Janna Hecker
Technical Editor: Sharon Crawford
Word Processors: Scott Campbell and Lisa Mitchell
Book Designer: Elke Hermanowski
Icon Designer: Helen Bruno
Screen Graphics: Cuong Le
Desktop Production Artists: Ingrid Owen and Lisa Jaffe
Proofreader: Barbara Dahl
Indexer: Ted Laux
Cover Designer: Archer Design
Screen reproductions produced by XenoFont.

Acknowledgments

A book is always a joint effort. I would like to acknowledge Intuit for providing the Quicken 4.0 software; Steve Cummings, the author who did such a nice job on *Understanding Quicken 4;* Gene Weisskopf, whose input proved helpful at the onset of this project; Dianne King, who has kept me busy in spite of myself; Joanne Cuthbertson, who guides the Up and Running series; Marilyn Smith, my favorite editor/co-worker; Janna Hecker, who skillfully coordinated the project; and the entire SYBEX team noted on the copyright page.

SYBEX
Up & Running Books

The Up & Running series of books from SYBEX has been developed for committed, eager PC users who would like to become familiar with a wide variety of programs and operations as quickly as possible. We assume that you are comfortable with your PC and that you know the basic functions of word processing, spreadsheets, and database management. With this background, Up & Running books will show you in 20 steps what particular products can do and how to use them.

*Who
this book
is for*

Up & Running books are designed to save you time and money. First, you can avoid purchase mistakes by previewing products before you buy them—exploring their features, strengths, and limitations. Second, once you decide to purchase a product, you can learn its basics quickly by following the 20 steps—even if you are a beginner.

*What
this book
provides*

The first step usually covers software installation in relation to hardware requirements. You'll learn whether the program can operate with your available hardware as well as various methods for starting the program. The second step often introduces the program's user interface. The remaining 18 steps demonstrate the program's basic functions, using examples and short descriptions.

*Contents
&
structure*

A clock shows the amount of time you can expect to spend at your computer for each step. Naturally, you'll need much less time if you only read through the step rather than complete it at your computer.

*Special
symbols
and notes*

You can also focus on particular points by scanning the short notes in the margins and locating the sections you are most interested in.

In addition, three symbols highlight particular sections of text:

The Action symbol highlights important steps that you will carry out.

The Tip symbol indicates a practical hint or special technique.

The Warning symbol alerts you to a potential problem and suggestions for avoiding it.

We have structured the Up & Running books so that the busy user spends little time studying documentation and is not burdened with unnecessary text. An Up & Running book cannot, of course, replace a lengthier book that contains advanced applications. However, you will get the information you need to put the program to practical use and to learn its basic functions in the shortest possible time.

We welcome your comments

SYBEX is very interested in your reactions to the Up & Running series. Your opinions and suggestions will help all of our readers, including yourself. Please send your comments to: SYBEX Editorial Department, 2021 Challenger Drive, Alameda, CA 94501.

Preface

Quicken 4.0, from Intuit, is a checkwriting software package that also manages credit card accounts and investments. Quicken is a best-seller because you don't have to know accounting to keep track of what you owe, what you spend, and what you own. Its many reports, including a balance sheet, budget variance, and tax summary, reveal your financial position at any time.

Up and Running with Quicken 4 is a fast-paced guide to this popular financial management software. It concisely covers the major functions of the program so you can get going with the least amount of study.

If you are already using Quicken 3, this book will simplify your transition to Quicken 4.0. You can quickly learn how to use the new features. If this is your first experience with Quicken, you will soon understand the program and be writing checks and budgeting in no time.

Table of Contents

Step 1

Installation

Before you can use the program, you must first install it and set some parameters. This step takes you through installing and setting up Quicken.

Hardware Requirements

You can install Quicken 4 on a hard disk or floppy disk computer system, although a hard disk is usually preferable. The hardware requirements are as follows:

- An IBM PC, XT, AT, PS/2, or compatible computer
- DOS 2.0 or later
- 320K RAM (384K RAM with DOS 3.0 or later)
- One floppy disk drive, either 3½- or 5¼-inch
- Monochrome or color, 80-column monitor

If you want to print checks or reports, you will also need access to a printer.

Preparations

To protect your original disks, make copies of them, and then use the new working copies to install and run the program. In preparation, format either one blank 3¼-inch disk or two 5½-inch disks and label them to match the original Quicken disks.

Back up the original disks.

You can use the DOS command DISKCOPY A: B: to duplicate the original disk (placed in drive A) on a blank, formatted disk (placed in drive B). If you have only one drive, the source drive and the target drive in the command will be the same (DISKCOPY A: A:), and you will have to switch disks when prompted. After you duplicate the original disks, store them in a safe place.

Installing on a Floppy Drive

You can install Quicken on a dual or single floppy disk drive computer. In either case, you should format three blank disks before beginning the installation.

The following steps outline how to install Quicken on a computer with two floppy disk drives. Installation on a single floppy disk system is similar; follow the instructions on the screen. Note that at any time during the installation, you can press Esc to cancel the process.

1. Place the Quicken Disk 1, the Install/Startup disk, in drive A.

2. Place a blank, formatted disk in drive B.

3. At the A: prompt, type **install**, and then press Return. If you have a color monitor, when the information screen appears, press F2 to change the monitor setting to color.

4. At the information screen, press Return to continue. You will see the prompt

   `Install Quicken onto:`

5. Enter **2** if you have two floppy disk drives and will be installing on drive B.

6. Press Return at the next prompt to verify that you have a blank, formatted disk in drive B. The message

   `Installing Quicken`

   appears, followed by a screen that tells you the disk in drive B will be called the Installed Quicken Startup/Help Disk.

7. Press Return to continue. The Installing Quicken message reappears, and then you are instructed to change disks.

8. Remove the Quicken Disk 1 from drive A, replace it with the Quicken Program Disk 2, and press Return. The Installing Quicken message reappears, and then you are asked to insert another blank, formatted disk in drive B, which you will call the Installed Quicken Program Disk.

9. Remove the first disk from drive B and label it Disk 1, Start Up Disk.

10. Place a second, blank, formatted disk in drive B and press Return to continue. The Installing Quicken message reappears. When the process is complete, you are notified and reminded to send in your registration card.

11. Remove the disk from drive B and label it Disk 2, Program Disk.

Store your original disks in a safe place and use the copied disks as your working disks.

Installing on a Hard Drive

If you have a hard disk, you can optionally also install *Billminder,* a Quicken program that reminds you when items you've recorded in Quicken are due. (It adds a line to your AUTOEXEC.BAT file so that the reminders appear when you turn on the computer.)

To install Quicken on a hard disk computer, follow the steps below. Note that you can press Esc at any time during installation to cancel the process.

1. Place Disk 1, the Install/Startup disk, in drive A.

2. Type A:, and then press Return to change to drive A.

3. Type **install,** and then press Return. An information window appears. If you have a color monitor, press F2 to change the display to a color setting.

4. Press Return to continue. You will see the prompt

    `Install Quicken onto:`

5. Enter **3** to install Quicken on your hard drive.

6. When you are prompted to specify your drive and directory, enter the drive letter and name of the directory where you want to load the Quicken program. The default is C:\QUICKEN4.

The program will create the directory you specify if it does not already exist. If you are converting from an earlier version of Quicken, the new program files will replace the earlier ones in the same directory, or you can specify a separate directory for the latest version.

7. When you are prompted

    Do you want Billminder to be installed?

    enter **Y** or **N**. (If you install Billminder, you can deactivate it using the Other Settings option on the Change Settings menu.) The program displays a message indicating that Quicken is being installed, and then you are prompted

    Please insert the original QUICKEN 4.0 PROGRAM DISK in drive A.

8. Remove Disk 1 from drive A, replace it with Disk 2, and press Return. The installation process will continue; you will be notified when it is completed.

9. Press Return to exit from the installation process.

When you install Quicken, the program sets or creates the CONFIG.SYS files and buffers to meet Quicken specifications. It also creates a Q.BAT file in the root directory (renaming any existing file of the same name to QOLD.BAT). Thus, you can start Quicken from the root directory, without first changing to the Quicken directory.

Starting Quicken

After installing the program, you start Quicken by typing **Q** at the DOS prompt. If you have a floppy disk computer, you must first place Disk 1, your Startup disk, in drive B before you type Q. You also will be asked to replace the Startup disk with the Program disk after you select a Main menu option, and to insert a blank, formatted, data disk at the appropriate time.

If you have a color adapter card but ignored the color monitor prompt during installation, the first time you start the program, you are asked

Do you have a color monitor?

Use the arrow keys to select Yes or No, and then press Return.

The default monitor setting is for a fast monitor. If you have a slow monitor, such as an LCD screen on a laptop computer, use the Monitor Speed option on the Change Settings menu to reset the speed. This setting is discussed later in this step. Press Return to continue.

The Main menu appears whenever you start the program. The options on the Main menu are discussed in the next step.

Hardware Settings

To complete your setup of the program, you should consider the hardware settings, as well as several other choices that are noted in the following sections.

Monitor Settings

You control the monitor using the Screen Colors and Monitor Speed options on the Change Settings menu. Quicken differentiates between "fast" and "slow" monitors. The default is fast, but if you have problems reading the screen, try the slow setting. If you have a monochrome monitor, you can choose between the Monochrome or Shades of Gray color settings. With a color monitor, your choices are Navy/Azure, White/Navy, or Red/Gray.

Printer Settings

You can print three types of documents in Quicken: checks, reports, and alternate reports. These documents can be directed to separate printers or one printer with a different format set up for each type.

The default printer is set for 10 characters per inch and is connected to the parallel printer port LPT1. To define your printer, follow these steps:

1. Select the Change Settings option from the Main menu.

2. Choose Printer Settings from the Change Settings submenu.

3. Select Check Printer Settings to display the list of printers.

4. Choose your printer by moving the cursor to it and pressing Return.

Quicken provides settings for a few models of a limited number of printer manufacturers and three generic categories: IBM Compatibles, Unlisted Printer, and Unlisted Laser. You can also enter your printer's name and the required data from your printer manual.

You can return to this list and select another printer or change the printer parameters. Step 15 explains printer parameters in more detail.

Other Settings

Quicken allows you to make choices regarding other settings in the program. The choices and their default settings appear when you select the Other Settings option on the Change Settings menu, as shown in Figure 1.1.

Leave the default settings or make changes based on your preferences. Most choices require a yes or no response. Other possible responses are shown on screen beside the prompt.

When you have moved partially down the Other Settings list and want to accept the defaults for the remaining questions, press Ctrl-Return.

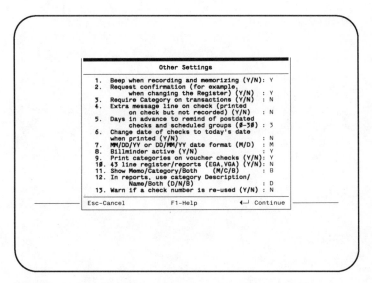

```
                    Other Settings
    1.  Beep when recording and memorizing (Y/N): Y
    2.  Request confirmation (for example,
          when changing the Register) (Y/N)   : Y
    3.  Require Category on transactions (Y/N)  : N
    4.  Extra message line on check (printed
          on check but not recorded) (Y/N)    : N
    5.  Days in advance to remind of postdated
          checks and scheduled groups (Ø-3Ø)  : 3
    6.  Change date of checks to today's date
          when printed (Y/N)                  : N
    7.  MM/DD/YY or DD/MM/YY date format (M/D)  : M
    8.  Billminder active (Y/N)                 : Y
    9.  Print categories on voucher checks (Y/N): Y
    1Ø. 43 line register/reports (EGA,VGA) (Y/N): N
    11. Show Memo/Category/Both    (M/C/B)      : B
    12. In reports, use category Description/
          Name/Both (D/N/B)                   : D
    13. Warn if a check number is re-used (Y/N) : N

    Esc-Cancel          F1-Help          ◄─┘ Continue
```

Figure 1.1: Other settings in Quicken

You may want to wait until you become more familiar with the program before changing its other settings.

Upgrading from Quicken 3

If you are upgrading from Quicken 3, press Esc to return to the Main menu. Press Ctrl-G, then F9, and you will be prompted to enter the name of the directory where your data is stored.

Loading Categories

You can use Quicken for keeping track of and categorizing personal (home) financial activities or activities in your business. Quicken provides standard categories for home and business income and expenses, as listed in Table 1.1. You can add to, delete from, and edit the default lists if you choose to use them.

Default Home Categories

Income

Bonus Income
Canadian Pension
Dividend Income
Family Allowance
Gift Received
Interest Income
Investment Income
Old Age Pension
Salary Income

Expenses

Automobile Fuel
Auto Loan Payment
Automobile Service
Bank Charge
Charitable Donations
Childcare Expense
Christmas Expense
Clothing
Dining Out
Dues
Education
Entertainment
Gift Expense
Groceries
Home Repair & Maintenance
Household Miscellaneous Expense
Housing
Insurance
Interest Expense
Investment Expense

Table 1.1: Income and Expense Categories Supplied by Quicken

Default Home Categories

Expenses

Medical & Dental
Miscellaneous Expense
Mortgage Interest Expense
Mortgage Principal
Other Expenses
Recreation Expense
Reg Retirement Savings Plan
Subscriptions
Supplies
Federal Tax
Social Security Tax
Miscellaneous Taxes
Property Tax
State Tax
Telephone Expense
Unemployment Insurance
Water, Gas, Electric

Default Business Categories

Income

Gross Sales
Other Income
Rent Income

Expenses

Advertising
Car & Truck
Freight
Interest Paid

Table 1.1: Income and Expense Categories Supplied by Quicken (continued)

Default Business Categories

Expenses

Legal & Professional Fees
Late Payment Fees
Office Expenses
Rent Expense
Repairs
Returns & Allowances
Taxes
Travel Expenses
Wages & Job Credits

Table 1.1: Income and Expense Categories Supplied by Quicken (continued)

This is an important decision.

If you are not upgrading from Quicken 3, you need to indicate which categories of data you want to use and where to store the data. If you are upgrading, you can skip the selection.

After you set up your monitor, printer, and other settings, follow these steps to set up categories:

1. Press Esc to return to the Main menu.

2. Choose the Select Account option. You are prompted

    `Standard categories to use:`

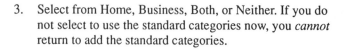

3. Select from Home, Business, Both, or Neither. If you do not select to use the standard categories now, you *cannot* return to add the standard categories.

If you intend to transfer monies from home to business or vice versa, or you want to use a mixture of the predefined categories in either home or business, select Both. The categories will be inter-mixed alphabetically. You can use any category in any transaction. However, a category should be devoted solely to either home or business transactions.

If you select Neither, you must create your own categories to classify your transactions. See Step 3 for information about creating, editing, and deleting categories.

4. At the next prompt

    `Location for data files:`

    accept the default of the drive and directory for your
    Quicken program, or enter another drive and/or
    directory. Quicken creates a subdirectory with the name
    QDATA for the files within the directory you indicate.

Next, you are prompted to set up the types of accounts you will need. You must set up at least one bank account. Read Step 4 for information about creating accounts.

Passwords

You can establish a main password that restricts access to all the Quicken functions, as well as a transaction password that restricts editing transactions dated earlier than the password allows.

To set up or change passwords, select Change Settings from the Main menu, then Passwords from the submenu. Choose to create a main or transaction password. Type a password of up to 16 characters, and then enter the same password a second time to confirm it. When you create a transaction password, you specify the date the transactions must be later than before the user can gain access to them.

The *user interface* is how you communicate with Quicken. The program's menus, function keys, and Control (Ctrl)-key combinations are described in this step.

The Main Menu

You begin your Quicken session, and you should end your work, at the Main menu. One of the options on this menu is Exit. It is the only graceful way to leave the program. If you turn the computer off or there is a power failure before you select the Exit option, you could damage your files.

Here is a brief summary of each option on Quicken's Main menu:

- Write/Print Checks: Use this option to create and print checks for your expenses or to submit payments electronically to your creditors.

- Register: Use this option to view or change existing transactions or to record transactions that are not generated by the computer.

- Reports: Use this option to create reports or print them.

- Select Account: Use this option to create accounts or work with existing accounts.

- Change Settings: Use this option to control hardware settings and a few program parameters such as passwords, or to reach the Account Group Activities menu.

- Exit: Use this option to exit the Quicken program and return to DOS.

Accessing Menus, Options, and Functions

A few of the Main menu options display a submenu. There are also six pull-down menus that you access by pressing a function key. These menus are on the inside cover of this book. To select an option on a menu, press the key listed beside it. You can also use the up and down arrow keys to move the cursor to an option and then press Return to select it.

When you display a list of items, such as a category list, you must use the up and down arrow keys to move the cursor to the item you want to choose, and then press Return to select it.

The Pull-Down Menus

A pull-down menu bar appears across the top of your screen when you are writing checks or using a register. The following pull-down menus are provided:

Press F1 anywhere in the program to display Help text.

- Help: Press F1 to display Help text specific to the current screen or field. Press F1 within the Help text to display the list of topics for which help is available. Use the up and down arrow keys to move the cursor to the topic you want to read about and press Return to display the related text. Press Esc to return to processing.

- Acct/Print: Press F2 to select or set up an account; print checks or the transactions in a register; change printer settings; back up your account data; import or export data; or transmit payments.

- Edit: Press F3 to find and edit transactions or transmit stop payments and payment inquiries.

- Quick Entry: Press F4 to memorize and recall transactions; set up or select categories and classes; set up or select an electronic payee; select a transaction group to process; set up or select a security; or select an investment action.

- Reports: Press F5 to select a report to process.

- Activities: Press F6 to write checks; reconcile check and credit card accounts; adjust a cash or investment balance; update investment prices; order supplies from Quicken; access the calculator or DOS; or send electronic mail to CheckFree.

You can bypass the submenu and access a submenu option by pressing the appropriate Ctrl-key combination. The options on a pull-down menu vary depending on the type of account you are working with.

Ctrl-Key Combinations

Throughout the program, you can use Ctrl-key combinations to quickly access functions. Quicken uses the same key combinations for several functions. The function you access depends on where you are in the program. Several Ctrl-key combinations are applicable when the pull-down menu bar is displayed across the top of the screen. Other Ctrl-key combinations are displayed at the bottom of the screen when they are available. Still other key combinations are noted only in the Help text.

Ctrl-key combinations give quick access to functions.

A list of Ctrl keys and the functions they access appears on the inside cover of this book.

Entering Data

Entering data in Quicken is similar to entering data in most up-to-date software. The keyboard, the numeric keypad, function keys, and other control keys work as you might expect.

You can use the following keys to move the cursor:

Home	Moves to the top of the screen
End	Moves to the bottom of the screen
Page Up	Moves to the previous screen
Page Down	Moves to the next screen
Up arrow	Moves up one line
Down arrow	Moves down one line
Tab forward	Moves forward one field
Tab backward	Moves backward one field

Recording Data in a Field

As you type, Quicken places the new character above the cursor, and moves existing characters to the right (as if the Insert function were on). You can use the following keys as you enter data:

- The Delete key erases the character above the cursor and closes the space.

- The Backspace key erases the character to the left of the cursor and closes the space.

- The Return key records data you have typed in a field and moves the cursor forward to the next field.

Entering Dates

By default, Quicken will supply the current date for all entries, but you can override it. Use the + key to move the date forward one day at a time, or the − key to move backward one day at a time. You can also enter the specific date you want to use, in *MM/DD/ YY* format. Usually, you must include the slashes in your dates. For example, February 7, 1991, is entered **02/07/91**.

Entering Dollar Amounts

Quicken records all amounts as whole dollars, unless you indicate otherwise. To record cents, you must enter the decimal point between the dollars and the cents. For example, if you want to enter one thousand sixty-seven dollars, type **1267**. Quicken records it as $1267.00. To enter twelve dollars and sixty-seven cents, type **12.67.**

In order to be used to enter numbers, the ten-key pad must be a dedicated numeric pad, or the NumLock function must be on. Otherwise, you must enter numbers from the main keyboard.

Saving Your Entries

When the cursor moves through the last field on a screen, the entry is saved automatically. You can also press F10 at any point in a completed entry to save it and skip the remaining fields.

Changing or Deleting Data

Almost everything you do or enter in Quicken can be changed, even after you have saved it. This includes check amounts, account names, and transaction amounts. You can delete transactions even after they are completed.

The problem with this flexibility is that there is no *audit trail*—no record of what went before. For your home finances, this may be fine, but for a set of business books, it is not accepted accounting practice.

To change a transaction, simply type over what exists in the fields and select to save the changes. You can also redefine a record such as a bank account title or the tax status for a category. To do so, highlight it on the account or category list, then press Ctrl-E, change the data, and press F10 to save the modified record. To delete a transaction, press Ctrl-D, and then confirm the deletion.

Glossary

It is not necessary to know accounting terms or concepts to use Quicken. However, Quicken has its own set of terms that you should understand:

Become familiar with Quicken's set of terms.

- *Account:* An individual record in which you keep related transactions.

- *Account group:* A collection of accounts you have stored in a specific directory.

- *Account type:* One of six types of accounts defined by Quicken: bank, credit card, cash, investment, other liability, or other asset.

- *Assets:* Items you own or money owed to you.

- *Bank account:* An account type that tracks transactions in a checking, savings, or money market account.

- *Beginning balance:* The balance in an account or on a statement before all the transactions appearing on it have been accounted for.

- *Budget:* A preset amount you expect to receive or spend for a specific category.

- *Cash:* An account type that keeps track of transactions involving actual dollar bills and coins instead of checks.

- *Category:* A means of generically classifying your transactions for grouping on reports.

- *Class:* A means of further separating your transactions by very specific definitions.

- *Credit card:* An account type that tracks transactions charged to a credit card.

- *Current balance:* The balance in an account as of the current date, which does not include transactions recorded with a future date.

- *Custom report:* A report that allows selection of specific records in the data files.

- *Ending balance:* The balance in an account after all recorded transactions have been considered.

- *Filter:* A method of excluding records that do not meet your selection criteria from a report.

- *Investment:* An account type that keeps track of transactions involving investments.

- *Liability:* Money you owe.

- *Memo:* A notation on a check or transaction that can appear on the printed check and be used as selection criteria in a report.

- *Memorize:* To store a transaction that occurs repeatedly so you can copy it in the future.

- *Opening balance:* The balance of an account when you first define it in Quicken.

- *Other asset:* Tangible items you own.

- *Other liability:* What you owe on large items or money you borrowed.

- *Payee:* The person or company to whom a check is written.

- *Register:* A listing of the transactions that have affected a given account.

- *Split transaction:* A transaction that charges the amount to more than one category.

- *Subcategory:* Further defines a category.

- *Subclass:* Further defines a class.

- *Transaction:* An activity that increases or decreases your account balance, for each individual record.

- *Transaction group:* Several recurring transactions that you place in a group and recall for processing all at one time.

- *Transfer:* A movement of monies between accounts.

Step 3

Creating Accounts

In order to record your transactions in Quicken, you must first set up your accounts. This step describes how to create and maintain accounts.

Account Types and Groups

Quicken keeps track of your financial activity by account type in account groups. There are six *account types:*

There are six account types.

- Bank account: Identifies your checking, savings, or money market accounts. Enter the ending balance from your bank statement and the date of the statement.

- Credit card: Identifies the various charge cards you use. Enter the balance due from your most recent statement and the closing date. You can also record your credit limit.

- Cash: Records expenditures made in the form of cash, such as money in your wallet or the petty cash fund in your business. Enter the amount of cash you have on hand as of the date you are establishing your records and that date.

- Other asset: Identifies large items you own, such as your home or automobiles. In a business, this would include assets other than cash, such as accounts receivable or equipment. Enter the value of the asset and the date of the valuation. This account type is discussed in Step 7.

- Other liability: Records your debts, such as a home mortgage or car loan. In a business, this would include all the small purchases for which the vendor extended you payment terms. Enter the amount you owe and the date. This account type is also discussed in Step 7.

- Investment account: Keeps track of your purchase, sale, and profit or loss on investments, such as mutual funds, bonds, or collectibles. Investment accounts are detailed in Step 8.

An *account group* is a collection of the six possible account types with its own set of categories and transactions. Within each account type, you can have several accounts.

An *account* is an individual record in which you record related transactions. For example, under bank accounts, you might have a checking account, a savings account, a Christmas club account, and perhaps a money market account. You record *transactions,* which are activities that increase or decrease your account balance, for each individual account. In a bank account, typical transactions are deposits, checks, and service charges.

Setting Up Accounts

To set up an account, follow these steps:

1. Choose Select Account from the Main menu.

A sample account group is shown in Figure 3.1. In this example, the default drive and directory were not used to store the account group. Instead, Quicken was installed on drive D in a directory named QK. The subdirectory, QDATA, is the program default.

2. Use the Home key to move the cursor to the New Account option at the top of the account list, and then press Return.

3. Enter the number which represents the type of account you want to establish; for example, enter 2 for credit cards.

4. Enter an abbreviated name for the account (15 characters maximum); for example, enter the name of the credit card company, a money market fund number, or a loan number.

5. Enter the balance of the account. Remember to type a decimal point between dollars and cents, as in 980.34.

6. Enter the date that balance was accurate (override the default system date if necessary).

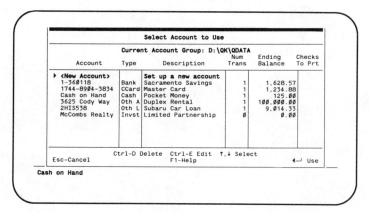

```
                        Select Account to Use

                 Current Account Group: D:\QK\QDATA
                                              Num    Ending    Checks
        Account      Type       Description   Trans  Balance   To Prt

  ▶ <New Account>            Set up a new account
    1-360118         Bank   Sacramento Savings    1   1,628.57
    1744-8904-3834   CCard  Master Card           1   1,234.88
    Cash on Hand     Cash   Pocket Money          1     125.00
    3625 Cody Way     Oth A  Duplex Rental        1  100,000.00
    2HIS538          Oth L  Subaru Car Loan       1   9,014.33
    McCombs Realty   Invst  Limited Partnership   0       0.00


              Ctrl-D Delete   Ctrl-E Edit   ↑,↓ Select
    Esc-Cancel                F1-Help                      ←┘ Use

  Cash on Hand
```

Figure 3.1: A sample account group

7. Optionally, enter a full description of the account (20 char-
    acters maximum); for example, Citibank VISA or your
    credit card number. For a credit card account, you can also
    record your credit limit.

The program redisplays the list of accounts, with the new account
included in alphabetical order within its account type.

Recording Activity

There are three ways to record activity in an account. In a bank
account, the most common entry is made by writing a check. In
all other account types, you typically enter a transaction in the
account register. The third way transactions are recorded in an account are via a transfer from another account; for example, you
make a payment on your credit card with a check written on your
bank account. Using account registers is discussed in Step 5.

Step 4

Defining Categories

15

Within Quicken, you can separate your transactions into categories and classes, and even subcategories and subclasses. This separation allows you to classify your transactions in ever-increasing detail, for your own budgeting, as well as for income tax reporting.

Classifying with Categories

A *category* is a means of classifying your transactions for grouping on reports. For example, you can print a list of all the money you spent on telephone bills. As explained in Step 1, Quicken supplies default categories, and you choose whether or not to use them during setup. You can also add to the list or create your own categories.

Use Quicken categories to group your expenses and income.

Quicken's category and transfer list is consisted of two kinds of information:

- The income and expense categories you use to classify your financial transactions

- Accounts you have established, such as your bank or liability account, so that you can transfer funds between the accounts

Adding Categories

To add a new category, follow these steps:

1. Select Register from the Main menu.

2. Press F4 (*Quick Entry*) and select Categorize/Transfer from the submenu to display the list of categories. (You can also display the category and transfer list by pressing Ctrl-C when the cursor is in a transaction's Category field.)

3. When the category and transfer list appears, press the Home key to move the cursor to the New Category field at the top of the list.

4. Press Return to add a new category. Quicken displays the Set Up Category window.

5. Enter a name (15 characters maximum) for the category.

6. For Type, enter **I** to set up an income category, or **E** to set up an expense. Subcategories are discussed in the next section.

7. In the Description field, you can enter a longer description of the item (25 characters maximum) if you had to abbreviate in the Name field.

8. In the Tax-related field, enter **Y** if transactions charged to this category are used for income tax reporting.

When you complete the last field, the new category is added to the list in alphabetical order within its type. Income categories are listed first, expense categories second, subcategories third, followed by bank accounts, credit card accounts, cash accounts, other asset accounts, other liability accounts, and, finally, investment accounts.

You can set up your categories in advance or while you are entering a transaction. To define a new category during data entry, simply type its name in the Category field and press Return. Quicken notifies you that the category is not found. Select Add to Category List and complete the fields in the Set Up Category window.

You determine whether or not Quicken will force you to enter a category for each transaction when you respond to the prompt

```
Require Category on transactions
```

displayed by the Other Settings option. You also select if the category name, the category description, or both will appear on reports and in the register through the Other Settings option.

Editing and Deleting Categories

You can change the name, type, description, or tax notation of an existing category. To edit a category, highlight it, press Ctrl-E to display the Edit Category screen, and type the new definition. Press F10 to record the changes.

You can also delete an existing category. For example, if you selected to use Quicken's predefined categories, you may want to delete some unnecessary ones. To delete a category, highlight it, press Ctrl-D, and then confirm that you want to delete the item.

When you delete a category, it is removed from all previous transactions in which it was used, leaving them uncategorized.

Setting Up Subcategories

Subcategories further define categories. For example, the Medical & Dental category could be divided into Doctor, Dentist, Optometrist, and Hospital subcategories. With this definition, you could report on your total medical and dental expenses, and then determine the amount you spent just on doctor bills.

The subcategory is not assigned to a primary category in the category definition. Instead, you join subcategories with a primary category during transaction entry. When you record a transaction, in the Category field, enter the primary category name, followed by a colon and the subcategory name. For example, to enter a transaction for a doctor bill, you might enter Medical:Doctor.

A subcategory stands alone; it can be used in combination with any primary category. For example, the subcategory Rent could be used with the primary category Housing to record apartment rent (Housing:Rent), or with Auto Service to record what it cost to rent a car while yours was being repaired (Auto Service:Rent).

To set up a subcategory, follow the steps to establish a category, but in the Income, Expense or Subcategory field, enter **S**. Subcategories can be used with either an Income or Expense type of transaction.

*Use classes
to further
define
transactions.*

Defining Classes

Categories and subcategories are usually sufficient to sort your transactions. However, you can further pigeonhole your transactions by classes. A *class* is a means of separating your transactions by very specific definitions, such as which family member spent money on lunch, or which car you bought gas for, or which apartment you were paying rent on.

When you enter a transaction, you can indicate the class by entering its name in the Category field, preceded by a slash (/). You can use a class in conjunction with a category or by itself.

Here are a few examples of how classes are used:

- Housing:Rent/Cody. This entry posts your transaction to your Housing category, in the Rent subcategory, for the Cody class, which is the apartment you rent on Cody Way.

- Housing:Rent/UCLA. This entry is for rent you pay on your son's dormitory at the university.

- /Cody. This entry is for any uncategorized expense for the apartment you live in on Cody Way.

Adding Classes

Quicken does not provide a default list of classes. To set up a class, follow these steps:

1. Select Register from the Main menu.

2. Press F4 (*Quick Entry*) and choose Select/Set Up Class from the submenu to display the list of classes. (You can also display the class list by pressing Ctrl-L when the cursor is in the Category field in a transaction.)

3. When the class list appears, press the Home key to move the cursor to the New Class field at the top of the list.

4. Press Return to add a new class. Quicken displays the Set Up Class window.

5. Enter a name (15 characters maximum) for the category.

6. In the Description field, you can enter a more detailed description of the class (25 characters maximum) if you had to abbreviate the name.

7. Complete the class description or press F10 after entering the name.

The new class is added to the class list. It appears in alphabetical order within the other classes.

You can also create *subclasses* to further define a class. Similar to a subcategory, a subclass is separated from the class by entering a colon between the two in the category field of a transaction. For example, to record a transaction for your son's dormitory rent for the spring quarter, you might enter Housing:Rent/UCLA:Spring.

You can edit or delete classes in the same way that you modify categories.

Printing Category and Class Lists

You can print both the category and transfer and class lists. Display the list as described in earlier sections, and then press Ctrl-P. Indicate which printer you want the report sent to. The list prints immediately, so have your printer ready. See Step 14 for more details on printing.

Preparing for April 15

Categories and classes are a handy way to separate transactions that you will report on income tax forms from those that you will not include. In preparation for April 15, set up categories and classes appropriate to the type of income tax forms you must complete. See which categories are on the various schedules you are required to send to the IRS. Then match the schedules and data you must provide with the categories and classes in your Quicken program.

For example, on the 1040 form, you must separate income received as wages from income received as interest. You must also separate personal income from income derived from owning a business. You would set up one category, Salary, and another category, Interest, for your personal transactions. Business activity should be kept in an entirely separate account group so you do not intermix business and personal transactions. Using Quicken in business is discussed in Step 19.

Set up your categories so that you can keep deductible and nondeductible expenses separate. When entering transactions, be careful not to mix deductible expenses with nondeductible expenses in the same category. For example, under Medical expense, you would enter costs for prescription drugs, but not for vitamins bought over the counter (unless the IRS changes the rules to include vitamins as a deductible expense). Nor would you typically include veterinarian bills in your Medical category. However, if you were using Quicken for your pedigreed cat business, you would be able to deduct veterinarian bills as a medical expense.

A *register* is a listing of the transactions that have affected a given account. Every account in each account type has its own unique register. Thus, there is an individual register for each bank, cash, credit card, liability, asset, and investment account. This step describes how to use the account register.

Contents of Account Registers

All transactions are entered into a register. There are two instances when Quicken automatically records transactions in the appropriate register for you: when you write a check, Quicken makes an entry in the bank account register, and when you originate a transfer in one account, Quicken makes an entry in the offsetting register.

Transactions are recorded in registers.

Fields in a register are displayed as column headings. Table 5.1 lists the fields common to most registers, and Tables 5.2 through 5.7 show those specific to particular account types.

Field	Description
Date	The date of the transaction. You can use dates to select transactions for reporting. You can also locate transactions in a register by date.
Ref	A five-character field where you can enter a brief identifier, such as the number of a cash receipt or sales slip (not available in a bank register).
Payee	The entity receiving a payment. You can use the payee to restrict data on reports.
Memo	A description of the transaction. You can use the memo to restrict data on reports. Memo notations can be printed on checks.

Table 5.1: Fields Common to Most Registers

Field	Description
Category	The category into which the transaction falls. You can use categories to restrict data on reports. Categories can be printed on voucher checks.
C	A column where you mark transactions, such as checks, as cleared (this field is not available in a cash register).
Balance	The remaining value of the account.

Table 5.1: Fields Common to Most Registers (continued)

Field	Description
Num	The check number or deposit slip number for the transaction. If you have written a check but not printed it, **** will appear. If you transmitted a payment via CheckFree, Quicken displays E-PMT in this field. If you have prepared a payment but have not yet transmitted it to CheckFree, Quicken displays >>>> beside the payment that is pending.
Payment	The amount of a payment originating in the bank account.
Deposit	The amount deposited to the bank account.

Table 5.2: Fields Specific to Bank Registers

Field	Description
Charge	An amount you charged to your credit card.
Payment	The amount you paid on your credit card.

Table 5.3: Fields Specific to Credit Card Registers

Field	Description
Spend	The amount of money you paid out of your cash account.
Receive	The amount of money you put into your cash account.

Table 5.4: Fields Specific to Cash Registers

Field	Description
Decrease	The amount by which the value of the asset decreased. This could be depreciation or a transaction to record the sale or disposal of an asset.
Increase	The amount by which the value of an asset increased. This could be appreciation or a transaction to record the purchase or acquisition of the asset.

Table 5.5: Fields Specific to Other Asset Registers

Field	Description
Increase	The amount by which the liability increased. This could be a transaction to record a loan you received.
Decrease	The amount paid against a liability.

Table 5.6: Fields Specific to Other Liability Registers

Field	Description
Action	A description of the type of transaction.
Security	The name of the security or investment.
Price	The price per share when buying or selling.

Table 5.7: Fields Specific to Investment Registers

Field	Description
Shares	The number of shares in the transaction.
Comm/Fee	The amount of a commision or fee related to the purchase or sale of shares.
$ Amount	The total amount of the current transaction.
Share Balance	The current value of the shares you hold.

Table 5.7: Fields Specific to Investment Registers (continued)

Transactions appear in the register in date order. If you *postdate* a transaction (give it a future date), Quicken places a double line beneath the current date and displays the transaction beneath the double line with its date highlighted.

Working in a Register

By working in a register, you can add new transactions, edit existing transactions, or view transactions in the account. To display the register of the current account, select Register from the Main menu.

To work in another register, press F2 (*Acct/Print*). When the account list appears, place the cursor on the account you want to work in, and press Return to select it. Quicken will display the register for the account you choose.

Entering Transactions

Fill in the account register fields to record a transaction.

You can move the cursor to the space beneath the last transaction in the account register to record a new transaction by pressing Ctrl-End. To enter a transaction, complete the fields that appear (see Tables 5.1 through 5.7 for a description of the fields).

When you complete the last field, Quicken asks if you want to record the transaction. Select Record Transaction, and Quicken will store your entry, sort it by date among the existing transactions, and calculate the new balance in the account.

Note that you do not record checks that you have written in the bank register, unless it is a check you wrote manually. Computer-generated checks are automatically entered in the register when you prepare them in Quicken (see Step 9).

As an example, the following steps are used to enter a transaction in a credit card account:

1. Select Register from the Main menu.

2. Press F2 (*Acct/Print*), and then choose Select/Set Up Account from the submenu to display the account list.

3. Highlight the account related to the transaction and press Return to select it.

4. In the Date field, enter the date the transaction took place, in the format *MM/DD*. If the transaction is for another year, follow the day with another slash and enter two digits for the year.

5. Enter a reference if applicable.

6. In the Payee field, enter the name of the company you paid with a credit card.

7. Enter the amount you charged in the Charge field.

8. Press Return through both the C (Cleared) and Payment fields.

9. Enter a notation in the Memo field to describe what you bought.

10. When the cursor moves to the Category field, press Ctrl-C to display the category list. You can also type in the name of the category if you know it.

11. Highlight the category appropriate to this transaction and press Return to select it.

12. Press Return to leave the Category field. Quicken asks

    OK to Record Transaction?

13. The cursor is on Record Transaction. Press Return to
continue.

Finding Transactions

All the transactions recorded in a register, for every year, remain
available for reporting or viewing until you remove them. You
can use the following quick keys to move around in an account
register:

Ctrl-Home	Moves to the very first entry in the register.
Ctrl-End	Moves past the last entry.
PgUp	Moves one screen up.
PgDn	Moves one screen down.
Ctrl-PgUp	Moves to the beginning of the previous month.
Ctrl-PgDn	Moves to the beginning of the next month.
Up arrow	Moves up one transaction.
Down arrow	Moves down one transaction.

You can also use the following options, which appear on the Edit
submenu:

- Find: Locates specific transactions per the search criteria
  you specify.

- Repeat Find, Backwards or Next: Looks either backward or
  forward for the next item that matches the search criteria.

- Go to Date: Locates transactions with the date you enter.

- Go to Transfer: Locates the offsetting transaction resulting
  from a transfer in the highlighted transaction. Transfers are
  identified by brackets around the entry in the Category
  field. Quicken displays the register for the account involved in the transfer and highlights that transaction. Transfers are discussed in Step 12.

To find a transaction using search criteria, press F3 (*Edit*), and then select Find from the submenu. You can search for entries in any of the input fields: Payee, Memo, Category, Num, Ref, and Amount. The program will search for exactly what you enter, but does not distinguish between uppercase and lowercase letters. For example, if you search for *act,* the program will locate *act, Act,* or *ACT,* but not *actual.*

Use search criteria to find specific transactions.

To locate a string of characters regardless of where they appear in the entry, you must precede and follow the characters with two dots. For example if you search for *..act..,* the program will find *act*ion, att*ract,* and inter*act*ive.

You can use the Cleared column to locate items that are or are not marked as cleared. Place an X in this column to locate cleared transactions, a period (.) to locate uncleared transactions, or an asterisk (*) to find recently cleared transactions.

Editing Transactions

One of the advantages of Quicken is that it places few restrictions on changing transactions after you have recorded them. You can revise, delete, void, and split existing transactions. To edit the transaction, move the cursor to the field you want to change, press Ctrl-Backspace to erase what exists in the field, and enter the new data. Press F10 to record the change.

You can make other changes using the options on the Edit submenu. Press F3 (*Edit*) to display a submenu with the following options:

- Record: Saves the transaction in the register and on the disk.

- Delete: Removes the transaction from the register and from the disk.

- Split: Assigns the transaction amount to two or more categories. Also used to enter a longer memo. (This option is discussed in Step 12.)

- Void: Retains a recorded transaction in the register and on disk, but marks it void, returns the amount to zero, and places an X in the Cleared column of the register.

To delete a transaction, highlight it, press F3 (*Edit*), and select Delete Transaction. You must verify that you do intend to erase the transaction. You can also press Ctrl-D to delete the highlighted transaction. When you delete a transaction, there will be no record that it ever existed. The only way to retrieve it is to restore a backup copy of your files that was made before the deletion took place.

You can delete cleared transactions; however, do so with caution. Your account may be out of balance the next time you attempt to reconcile it.

To void a transaction, highlight it, press F3 (*Edit*), and select Void Transaction. You can also press Ctrl-V to void the highlighted transaction. Quicken leaves the transaction in the register marked as VOID and places an X in the Cleared column to exclude it from the reconciliation process.

Printing Transaction Registers

To print a copy of the transactions in a register, press F2 (*Acct/Print*) when the register is displayed and select Print Register from the submenu. You can skip directly to the Print Register window by pressing Ctrl-P when the register is displayed.

At the prompt

        Print transactions from: to:

enter the first and last dates you want included on the report. The next prompt is

        Print to:

Select the destination of the report. The choices are Report Printer,

Alternate Report Printer, Check Printer, or Disk (which creates an ASCII file or a 1-2-3 file format).

You can, optionally, enter a heading to print at the top of the report. If you don't enter a title at the Title prompt, the name of the register will print as the title.

If you respond N at the prompt

Print one transaction per line (Y/N):

the transactions will print just as they appear in the register, with the Description, Memo, and Category fields on separate lines. If you enter Y to print one transaction per line, Quicken truncates the Payee, Memo, and Category fields, and all amounts are printed in one column, with negative values preceded by a minus sign.

If you want to print the detail for transactions that were split between several categories, respond Y to the prompt

Print transaction splits (Y/N):

The category and description with the related amount will be printed beneath the Payee and Memo notations.

The prompt

Sort by check number (Y/N):

is only applicable to bank accounts. The transactions will be sorted in check number sequence if you respond Y. Otherwise, they will be placed in date order.

The final prompt

Sort by reference number (Y/N):

is not applicable to bank or investment accounts. Respond Y if you want the transactions in other accounts sorted by the entry in the Ref field of the register. Otherwise, the transactions will be placed in date order.

Step 6

Cash and Credit Cards

15

Although most of your routine transactions will probably be handled through your checking account, you might also want to record some of your credit card and cash transactions. This step explains how to use Quicken to keep track of your credit card and cash activities. Setting up accounts is explained in Step 3.

Credit Card Accounts

Using plastic can be a real convenience, especially if you travel and don't want to carry cash. Quicken provides an easy way to keep track of your credit card charges so you don't suddenly find yourself in a deep financial hole.

Credit card accounts record the purchases, payments, and finance charges on your charge cards. You can set up as many accounts as you have credit cards, and each account will have its own register.

To keep on top of your charge accounts, you should enter the charges and payments in your credit card register as they occur. This way, you will always know what you owe. When your credit card statement arrives, you can reconcile it in much the same way you reconcile your checking account (see Step 11 for details).

At the time you reconcile your statement, while you are still thinking about it, you can enter a payment. The payment might be by a check you wrote manually, or by a check you will have Quicken generate later. You can also originate a payment from your bank account to your credit card account at any time. This transaction (a *transfer*) will appear in your credit card register automatically.

Figure 6.1 shows an example of a credit card register with a beginning entry of the balance due at the time Quicken was installed. Since then, a payment was made from the check account and three charges were entered.

Enter credit card charges to keep track of how much you owe.

```
F1-Help   F2-Acct/Print   F3-Edit   F4-Quick Entry   F5-Reports   F6-Activities

DATE  REF    PAYEE  ·  MEMO  ·  CATEGORY     CHARGE  C   PAYMENT    BALANCE

5/25       Opening Balance                  1,234 88 X            1,234 88
1991                       [1744-8904-383→]

6/10       Mellon Bank Master Card                      100 00    1,134 88
1991       Monthly Payment [1-360118]

6/14       Festive Frills                    156 94               1,291 82
1991       Summer's Prom D→Gifts

6/14       Nordstroms                        236 54               1,528 36
1991       Business Suit   Clothing

6/16       White Pelican Restaurant           98 00               1,626 36
1991       Father's Day      Dining

6/14  Memo:
1991   Cat :

1744-8904-3834                              Credit Remaining:$  873.64
Esc-Main Menu      Ctrl◄┘ Record            Ending Balance:  $1,626.36
```

Figure 6.1: Credit card transactions

Cash Accounts

Record pocket money or petty cash expenditures.

Cash accounts are one of the account types provided by Quicken. This type of account records actual cash you receive and spend. In a family, this usually is pocket money or lunch money each family member carries. In a business, you would use the cash account type to track the petty cash used for purchasing small items, such as coffee for the lunchroom.

Cash has a way of "slipping through our fingers" if we do not keep good records. Most of us have looked back at the end of a month and asked ourselves "Where did it all go?" Quicken will help answer this question if you put in a little effort. Keep the receipts when you pay in cash. Carry a small envelope in your wallet and put the receipts in it when you take the dollar bills out. At the end of the week, start Quicken and enter the receipts all at once. You can make one quick entry for the total week's activity in each category.

When you create a cash account, you can count the cash you have on hand and enter that as a beginning balance, or you can write a check to establish the new account.

You can transfer amounts from your bank accounts to your cash accounts and vice versa. For example, you might withdraw money from the automatic teller machine (ATM), or get "cash back" from a checking account deposit. Transfers create a transaction in the originating account and the receiving account.

In the example in Figure 6.2, the register shows the original money on hand when we started Quicken and money paid out of pocket for lunch, gas, and the children's allowances. We obtained cash from an ATM withdrawal.

The last transaction shown in the figure is a unique situation. Our teenager borrowed money to buy a car. The transaction was originally entered into Quicken as an asset account. The money owed to us is a form of accounts receivable. When the boy sent a check for his first payment, we cashed it and recorded the cash in our cash account. The entry is a transfer to the asset account, Loans Given. The transaction increases our cash, but it decreases the balance due to us on the loan and will show on the Loans Given register as such.

```
 F1-Help   F2-Acct/Print   F3-Edit   F4-Quick Entry  F5-Reports   F6-Activities

 DATE  REF   PAYEE  ·  MEMO  ·  CATEGORY    SPEND      RECEIVE    BALANCE

 6/ 1        Opening Balance                          125 ØØ    125 ØØ
 1991                   [Cash on Hand]

 6/16        Lunches week ending 6/15/91    27 88                 97 12
 1991                   Dining

 6/16        Gasoline week ending 6/15/91   11 92                 85 2Ø
 1991        174 miles      Auto Fuel

 6/16        Weekly allowances 6/16-6/22/91 16 ØØ                 69 2Ø
 1991        Kevin & Crystel Kid's Allowance

 6/16        ATM Withdrawal                           15Ø ØØ    219 2Ø
 1991                   [1-36Ø118]

 6/16        Clinton's June Payment                    5Ø ØØ    269 2Ø
 1991  Memo:
       Cat: [Loans Given]

 Cash on Hand
 Esc-Main Menu    Ctrl◄┘ Record              Ending Balance:  $269.2Ø
```

Figure 6.2: Cash transactions

Using the Calculator

Although you can use the calculator anywhere in the Quicken program, it is especially helpful in totaling cash receipts. As an example, let's add $21.30 and $13.78, and then subtract $4.50.

1. If you want to use the result of your calculations in a numeric field, before accessing the calculator, place the cursor in that field.

2. To use the calculator, press Ctrl-O. In the window that appears, you can add (+), subtract (−), multiply (*), and divide (/) amounts or calculate percentages (%).

3. Enter **21.30** followed by the + sign, because you are about to add the next figure to it.

4. Enter **13.78** followed by the − sign, because you are about to subtract the next figure.

5. Enter **4.50** and press Return to display the result.

6. Press F9 to paste the result of your calculation into the field.

7. If you are calculating an amount that is not to be used in the program, press Esc after obtaining your answer.

8. If you make an error, press C to clear the entire calculation and start over.

In our sample register in Figure 6.2, we used the calculator to total our lunch receipts for the week of June 15, and then pasted the results into the Spend column of the transaction.

Adjusting a Cash Account

You may not want to record every penny you spend. It is the rare person who keeps track of what each soft drink or candy bar costs. At the end of the week, you probably do not have enough receipts to cover all the cash that you spent. Quicken has foreseen this and provides a means of adjusting your cash account.

You do not reconcile a cash account as you would a checking or credit card account. Instead, use the Update Account Balance option on the Activities menu, as outlined in the steps below.

1. Choose Register from the Main menu.

2. Press F2 (*Acct/Print*), and select the cash account you want to balance.

3. When the register is displayed, press F6 (*Activities*).

4. Select Update Account Balances.

5. Enter the amount of cash you really have.

6. Enter the category for adjustments, such as cash overages and shortages. If you do not want to categorize the adjustment, leave the Category for Adjustment field blank.

Quicken will enter a transaction titled Balance Adjustment in the register and charge it to the category you indicate. Quicken enters the amount in the Spend or Receive column according to the difference between the balance in the register and the amount of cash you entered when you updated the account balance.

Step 7

Assets and Liabilities

Assets are items you own, and *liabilities* are items you owe. The money in your checking account qualifies as an asset, as does the cash in your cash account and the value of your investments. The amount you owe on your credit cards qualifies as a liability.

Quicken's account types define assets and liabilities somewhat differently, however. There are separate account types for your checking account, your credit cards, and your investments. Two account types, *other asset* and *other liability*, are reserved for specific kinds of items. Other asset accounts usually keep track of tangible assets, such as your automobile, television, or sterling silverware. Other liability accounts typically keep track of what you owe on these large items or money you borrowed. This step describes how to use other asset and other liability accounts.

Other Assets

Normally, the assets you record in Quicken are those that will have activity, such as depreciation or appreciation, so you can trace their decreasing or increasing value. It is quite simple to maintain a record of the cost of improvements on your home, which can be deducted from any capital gains taxes when you sell the house.

Record assets that depreciate or appreciate.

Many assets, such as your VCR, neither gain nor lose value in any notable amount. Therefore, you don't need to set them up as an account in Quicken because there is no activity to track. However, you might want to use Quicken as a database to list these valuables. Their values will be included in the calculation of your net worth. The list could also be useful if anything is stolen, lost in a fire, or to be disposed of according to your will.

Follow these steps to set up your other asset accounts:

1. Choose Select Account from the Main menu.

2. Move the cursor up to the New Account field and press Return to enter a new asset.

3. In the Account Type field, enter **4** for Other Asset.

4. Enter the name of the account (maximum of 15 characters).

5. In the Balance field, enter what the asset is worth today. Usually, you would enter the amount as whole dollars.

6. For the As Of date, enter the date the asset was worth the amount you entered in the Balance field.

7. You can, optionally, enter a more detailed description of the asset in the Description field (20 characters maximum).

When you press Return in the Description field, the asset is recorded. It will be sorted alphabetically by name in the other asset section of the account group list. If you want to make further entries in the asset record, move the cursor to the new account and press Return to display the related register. Making entries in a register is explained in Step 5.

Other Liabilities

Record your mortgage, car loan, and other large debts in an other liability account.

Liabilities reduce your net worth. Quicken helps you stay on top of these obligations. You will manage minor debts in your credit card accounts. Larger indebtedness is handled in other liability accounts. Quicken defines the mortgage on your house, the loan on your car, and the large amount you borrowed from Uncle Fred as other liabilities.

Follow these steps to set up your other liability accounts:

1. Choose Select Account from the Main menu.

2. Move the cursor up to the New Account field and press Return to enter the new liability.

3. In the Account Type field, enter **5** for Other Liability.

4. Enter the name of the account (maximum of 15 characters).

5. In the Balance field, enter the total amount you currently owe, including interest.

6. For the As Of date, enter the date the amount in the Balance field was accurate.

7. If you want to record more detailed information about the liability, enter it in the Description field (20 characters maximum).

When you press Return in the Description field, Quicken records the liability. It will appear in name order among the liabilities in the account group list. If you want to add more tranactions to your new account, move the cursor to the account's name in the list and press Return to display the related register. Making entries in a register is explained in Step 5.

If you use Quicken to generate a check to make a payment on a debt, enter the name of the liability account in the Category field when you prepare the check (see Step 9). Quicken will automatically make an entry in the liability account, noting the payment and reducing the amount in the Balance field of the register.

You cannot make a payment from the checking account and have it appear in the liability account as a transfer *and also* split the transaction to charge it to both principal and tax-deductible interest. In this case, you must make a separate entry in the liability register to record the reduction in your balance.

Step 8

Investment Accounts

Investment accounts identify each investment you have, such as stocks, bonds, or mutual funds. Quicken defines a single investment that has a value and usually a share price as a *security*. Investments also qualify as assets, but in Quicken you record securities in an investment account.

Setting Up an Investment Account

When you set up an investment account, you must indicate whether it is a single mutual fund or not. A single mutual fund is one that consists of one investment and no cash balance. If you have more than one security and a cash balance for an investment, Quicken does not consider it a mutual fund.

Set up investment accounts for your stocks, bonds, and mutual funds.

The following steps outline the procedure for setting up either a mutual fund or another type of investment account:

1. Choose Select Account from the Main menu and select New Account at the top of the screen.

2. Enter **6** as the account type you want to add.

3. Enter the name of the account.

4. Indicate if the account is a mutual fund or not.

5. Enter a more detailed description of the investment. After you identify the account, the program displays the Set Up Mutual Fund Security window if this is a mutual fund. If this is not a mutual fund, the account group list reappears, and you can skip to step 10 in this section.

6. When the Set Up Mutual Fund Security window appears, if you are going to import price information from a file, enter a symbol (up to 12 characters) for the security in the Symbol field.

7. Enter the kind of investment this is in the Type field. You can either press Ctrl-L to select from the list provided by Quicken (Bond, CD, Mutual Fund, or Stock), or choose Set Up New Type to create a new type when the list is displayed.

You can define up to eight security types. When you set up a type, you can select to treat its prices as decimals or fractions. You can use security types for reporting.

8. In the Goal field, you can indicate the purpose of the investment, or enter any other identifier you want to track. Press Ctrl-L to select from the list provided by Quicken (College Fund, Growth, High Risk, Income, or Low Risk), or create a new goal when the list is displayed.

You can define a maximum of eight goals. Security goals, like types, can be used for reporting.

9. Press Return after selecting a goal, and the current account group list will appear.

10. Move the cursor to your new investment and press Return to display the register. The First Time Setup window will appear. If this is a mutual fund, the Create Opening Share Balance window will appear. If this is not a mutual fund, press Return and skip to step 12 in this section.

After you define an investment account, you should enter its balance. Depending on whether or not you need historical detail, there are two ways to establish the account. You can record the opening balance with the accumulated number of shares and current price per share, or if you need more detailed information, you can record every transaction that has occurred, beginning with the date you acquired the fund or security.

11. To record only the share balance, enter the opening date, the number of shares held as of that date, and the price per share as of that date. Quicken will calculate the market value. To record historical detail, press Esc at the Create

Opening Share Balance window. The investment register will appear, and you can enter individual transactions. Skip to the next section to enter historical information.

12. In the Date column, enter the date you are setting up the investment account.

13. In the Action column, enter **ShrsIn** as the transaction.

14. In the Security column, enter the name of the security.

15. When the Security Not Found window appears, select to add your entry to the security list.

16. Complete the Symbol, Type, and Goal fields, as described in steps 6, 7, and 8 in this section.

17. In the Price column, enter the price per share as of the transaction date.

18. In the Shares column, enter the number of shares involved in this transaction. Quicken will compute the Amount field. Press Return.

19. You can enter a memo to describe the transaction, such as *Account Setup*.

20. At the Ok to Record Transaction window, select to record the transaction.

The next section explains how to enter existing transactions when you set up the account as well as how to record new transactions involving your investments.

Entering Historical and Daily Transactions

After you set up your investment account, you may want to enter existing transactions. You will definitely want to record new transactions that affect the investment over time. Both kinds of transactions are entered in the investment register. Figure 8.1 shows an example of historical data entered for a mutual fund. The fields in the investment register are summarized in Step 5. The following sections provide more details.

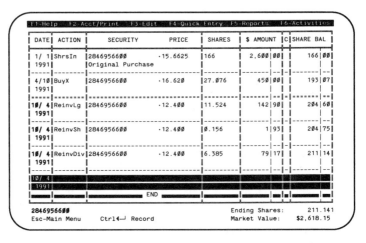

Figure 8.1: Entering historical detail in a mutual fund account

Actions in an Investment Register

In the Action field of the investment register, you can select from the following activities:

- Add or remove shares

- Buy shares

- Sell shares

- Receive dividends

- Distribute capital gains

  - Long-term

  - Short-term

- Reinvest returns into account

  - Dividends/income

  - Short-term gains

  - Long-term gains

- Other transactions

- • Reminder which works with Billminder

- • Miscellaneous expense

- • Return of capital

- • Stock split

- • Transfer cash

  - • Into account

  - • Out of account

- • Interest

  - • Interest income

  - • Margin loan interest payment

An action whose abbreviation appears in Quicken with a suffix of *X* involves the transfer of cash into or out of the account. Actions involving mutual funds are restricted to those that do not add or remove cash from the account.

Depending on the type of action you select, you can enter the price, number of shares, dollar amount, commission or fee, and transfer account. Quicken will calculate the ending shares and market value.

If this is a mutual fund, the name appears in the Security field; otherwise, you can enter the name of an existing security: press Ctrl-Y to select its name from a list of existing securities, or select New Security at the top of the list to add one.

The next three fields work in tandem. If you enter the price per share in the Price field and the number of shares in the Shares field, Quicken will calculate the dollar amount in the $Amount field. If you enter the price and the amount, Quicken will calculate the number of shares. Alternatively, you can enter the number of shares and the dollar amount, and Quicken will calculate the price per share. But before you make an entry in the Price or Shares field, you should be aware that Quicken defines prices and shares

*Your price
and share
amounts
depend on
the invest-
ment type.*

In the Price field, you should enter an amount as follows:

- The actual price for a stock or mutual fund share
- One-tenth of the actual market value for bonds (because prices are quoted in this manner)
- The total value of a CD, money market fund, or collectable
- The price per ounce of a precious metal

To record prices in fractions, enter the whole number, a space, and then the numerator and denominator of the fraction, separated by a slash; for example, 24 5/8. Quicken uses decimals to display prices, except for stock and bond prices, which are shown as fractions in sixteenths.

In the Shares field, enter the number of units as follows:

- The actual number of shares for a stock or mutual fund
- Ten times the actual number of bonds (in accord with the way prices are quoted)
- The number 1 for a CD, money market, or collectable
- The number of ounces for precious metals

You can also enter a notation in the Memo field to describe the transaction, such as *Original Purchase*. Quicken presents a window where you select whether or not to record the transaction. If you select not to, you can edit the current transaction before saving it.

Other Investment Information

If you enter a value in the Comm/Fee field, Quicken will add or subtract this figure from the total dollar amount of the transaction. Or Quicken will enter any difference between the total dollar amount and the price times the shares, assuming the difference to be a fee for the transaction.

Quicken makes transfer entries for certain investment transactions, such as buying or selling shares. For example, you must record where you are putting the money from a dividend: usually in your checking, savings, or cash account. You also need to indicate the account from which you are withdrawing money to buy shares. You can press Return to display your account list and select from it, or you can type the name of the account in the Account field.

Some investment transactions involve transfers.

Updating Prices and Adjusting Balances

If necessary, you can update a price in your investment account. While the investment register is displayed, press F6 (*Activities*), and then select Update Prices from the submenu. You can also press Ctrl-U to quickly access the update function. Quicken displays the Update Prices and Market Value screen for the current register and the current date.

The screen lists the type of security, the most recent market price recorded, the average cost per share, the percent of unrealized gain (an amount preceded by a minus sign indicates an unrealized loss), the number of whole shares you own, and the market value of the security.

To change the price, override the figure in the Mkt Price field. You can use the + or − keys to increase or decrease the price in one-eighth increments.

Update prices to keep your investment records current.

Selecting Dates and Accounts

From the Update Prices and Market Value screen, you can press F9 to toggle between one account and all accounts. When the list of all your investment accounts is displayed, move the cursor to the account you want to work with and change the price.

After you select the account, you can change the date and view market values for a date other than the current one. To do so, press Ctrl-G to go to a specific date, and enter that date in the field titled View Market Value As Of. Then enter the new price.

Another option is to display all the transaction dates for the security. Press Ctrl-H, and when the Price History screen appears, move the cursor to the date you want to change. You can then press Ctrl-D to delete the price, or press Ctrl-E to edit the existing price.

You can also add a date with price information to the Price History window. Move the cursor to the New Date option at the top of the list, press Return to display the New Price window, and enter the date and corresponding price.

Step 9

Preparing Checks

15

One of Quicken's major features is its capability to generate checks. Preparing checks is a two-step process:

1. Enter the amount of the check, the payee, and categorize the expense.

2. Print the check or electronically transmit the funds from your bank to the payee.

This step describes check preparation. Step 10 covers printing paper checks, and Step 17 addresses making electronic payments.

Follow these steps to write a check in Quicken:

1. To prepare a payment, choose Select Account from the Main menu and select the bank account upon which the checks will be drawn.

2. When the bank register appears, press Esc to return to the Main menu.

3. Select Write/Print checks, and a blank check form will appear.

4. Quicken supplies the system date as the check date. Press Return to accept the default, or enter another date. (You can print checks with current or future dates at any time.)

5. In the Pay to the Order Of field, enter the name of the person to whom you are writing the check. You can also recall a memorized check format to pay recurring obligations, as explained in Step 13.

6. Enter the amount of the check. The program will spell out the amount in the Dollars field.

7. You are allowed five lines for the street, city, state, and zip code. The address is situated to fit in the window envelopes available from Intuit.

If you press the quotation mark (") key in the first line of the address, Quicken fills in the payee name for you, and then you can enter the rest of the address.

8. You can make a notation of what you are paying in the Memo field. Your entry will be printed on the check.

9. In the Category field, you can assign the transactions to categories, subcategories, and classes. Type the name of an existing or new classification. Alternatively, you can select the entry from the category list (press Ctrl-C) or the class list (press Ctrl-L). Use the PgUp and PgDn or Home and End keys to scroll, highlight your choice, and then press Return to select it.

When the check is complete, it will look like the sample shown in Figure 9.1.

The check screen shows the account and balances.

The name of the bank account appears in the lower-left corner. The up arrow in the lower-right corner indicates checks written prior to this one are also pending. The down arrow indicates checks were written after this one. The dollar amount of checks awaiting printing appears in the Checks to Print field. The Current Balance is what the balance is today, without deducting for

```
 F1-Help   F2-Acct/Print   F3-Edit   F4-Quick Entry  F5-Reports   F6-Activities

    ┌──────────────────────────────────────────────────────────────────────┐
    │                                   Date    6/21/91                      │
    │ Pay to the                              ─────────                      │
    │ Order of    Student Education Travel Group          $ 1,000.00         │
    │                                                    ──────────          │
    │ One Thousand and 00/100********************************** Dollars       │
    │         ┌─────────────────────────────┐                                │
    │         │Attn: European Tour Department│                               │
    │         │P. O. Box 5916               │                                │
    │ Address │New York, NY 10163           │                                │
    │         │                             │                                │
    │ Memo  Deposit, Clint Oram                                              │
    └──────────────────────────────────────────────────────────────────────┘

       ┌───── Category ─────┐
       │Education           │
       └────────────────────┘                                           ↑↓
                                          Checks to Print: $1,371.00
    Bank of Arizona                       Current Balance: $1,004.00
    Esc-Main Menu      Ctrl↵  Record      Ending Balance:  $  729.00
```

Figure 9.1: The check format screen

postdated checks. The Ending Balance field shows the amount in the account after *all* pending checks have been deducted.

10. When you press Return in the Category field, you are asked

    OK to Record Transaction?

    Select not to record the check if you want to return and edit the entry. Otherwise, select to record the check, and the program will display a blank check form on the screen for entry of your next check.

Editing Checks Before Printing

At any time before you print your checks, you can change them. You can alter the data on the check, change the data in the bank register, or use the options on the Edit submenu.

Changing Information on the Check

Prior to printing, you can scroll through the checks and edit any of them. Make sure you are in the correct register, and then select Write/Print Checks from the Main menu. The account name appears in bold type in the lower-left corner of the screen. Use the PgUp and PgDn keys to scroll through the checks, or press F3 (*Edit*), and use the options on the Edit submenu to find the check.

Press F3 to edit a check.

When the check you want to edit appears on the screen, move the cursor to the field you want to change, press Ctrl-Backspace to erase what is in the field, and then type the new data. When you are finished making changes, press F10 to record the check.

Changing Data in the Register

Checks appear in the register as soon as you write them. The Num field in the register will contain asterisks (****) until the check is printed. You can change any information: the check date, payee, amount, memo, or category. Move the cursor to the field you want to change, press Ctrl-Backspace to erase the current entry, and type the new data. Press F10 to record the changes.

You can also use options on the Edit submenu, which you can access from both the check format and register screens by pressing F3 (*Edit*). The submenu options allow you to delete, void, or split transactions, as discussed in Step 5.

Completing the Process

After you prepare the checks, you must print them. Printing is covered in Step 10.

If you exit from the Quicken program without printing the checks you have written, Quicken will notify you that checks are pending the next time you start the program. As another reminder, an asterisk (*) appears in the Checks to Prt column on the account list. If you have a hard disk and are using Billminder, that utility will display a message reminding you about the pending checks whenever you turn on your computer.

Step 10

Printing Checks

Quicken handles three types of checks:

- Computer-generated and printed checks

- Manually written checks entered as transactions in the Quicken bank register

- Computer-generated checks transmitted electronically to CheckFree

Manual checks are addressed in Step 5, and electronic payments are discussed in Step 17. This step explains how to have Quicken print checks for you.

Check Styles

Quicken can print checks in five different styles:

- Regular: 8½-by-3½-inch check

- Wallet: 8½-by-3½-inch form—6-inch wide check, 2½-inch detachable stub on the left

- Voucher: 8½-by-7-inch form—3½-inch high check, 3½-inch detachable stub on the bottom

- Laser: 3½-inch check that fits the paper tray of a laser printer

- Laser voucher: Voucher-style check that fits the paper tray of a laser printer

Quicken provides five check styles.

You can set the printing on your checks to be either 10 or 12 characters per inch (cpi); the default setting is 10 cpi. Step 14 describes how to change the printer settings.

Printing Written Checks

Before you can use Quicken to print checks, you must first write them, as explained in Step 9. The steps below outline how to print the checks you have written.

1. To print written checks, select Write/Print Checks from the Main menu.

2. When the check format screen appears, press F2 (*Acct/ Print*), and then select the Print Checks option. The Print Checks window appears.

3. Press F8 (*Set Check Type*) to select the style of check to print: Regular, Wallet, Voucher, Laser, or Laser Voucher. If you use a laser printer, you can print additional copies (as duplicates for your records) by entering the number of copies. After making your selection, press Return to redisplay the Print Checks window.

Print a sample check to test the alignment.

4. If you need to test for alignment, press F9 (*Print Sample*).

If the test shows the checks are not aligned properly, the program will realign the printed data for you. There are line numbers on the pin-feed strip on the check. The alignment test prints a pointer line. Enter the line number that the pointer line is pointing to in the Position Number field. Quicken will immediately print a second test. Each check used for the test is voided.

5. When the checks are properly aligned, leave a blank in the Position Number field and press Return.

6. In the Print to field of the Print Checks window, enter the number of the printer you want to use to print the checks. You can send the checks to the report printer, the alternate report printer, or the check printer (see Step 15).

7. You can print all the pending checks by entering A in the Print All/Selected Checks field, or select specific checks by entering S. If you select to print all the checks, skip the next step below.

8. If you choose to print selected checks, a list of the checks you have written appears. They are all marked Print. Use the arrow keys to highlight the checks you *do not* want to generate, and then press the spacebar to remove the Print notation.

9. After selecting the checks to print, press Return and enter the number of the first check to be printed in the Next Check Number field. The checks will print immediately. After the checks are printed, you will see the prompt

    ```
    Did checks print OK?
    ```

10. If the checks printed properly, the process is complete. Press Return at the prompt. If they did not, or you change your mind after printing the checks, enter the number of the first check in the series that you want to cancel. The Print Checks window will reappear. From there, you can press Esc to cancel the check run.

If you cancel the check run, checks numbered before the number you enter are recorded; checks numbered after the canceled run remain as written but still pending printing.

Printing Postdated Checks

When you select to print checks, all the checks pending printing are included in the number of checks to print on the Print Checks window. However, if any of those checks are dated after the current date, a new field appears:

```
Print checks dated through:
```

with the current date as the default. The notation

```
There are xx postdated checks.
```

appears beneath the check date.

You can include postdated checks in the current run by entering a specific future date in the Print Checks Dated Through field. All

Specifying a future date to print post-dated checks.

checks with that or an earlier date will be generated. Another way to print postdated checks is to choose to print selected checks (by entering S in the Print All/Selected Checks field), move the cursor to a specific postdated check you want to print, and press the spacebar to mark it.

Listing Checks to Print

Print a list of pending checks.

Quicken can generate a list of all the checks you have written but not yet printed, which is called the A/P by Vendor report. Follow these steps to produce the report:

1. Select Reports from the Main menu. (You can also press F5 from the register or check format screen to access the Reports menu.)

2. Select Business Reports from the submenu.

3. Select A/P by Vendor. Optionally, enter a report title. The report will appear on the screen.

4. Press F8 (*Print*) if you want a paper copy of the list.

The report lists all unprinted checks by payee for all your bank accounts.

Step 11

Reconciling Accounts

As part of maintaining your accounts in Quicken, you will want to reconcile those accounts. This step describes the program's reconciliation feature for checking and savings, credit card, and investment accounts.

Reconciling Checking and Savings Accounts

Quicken has made the chore of balancing a checkbook a simple task. The following steps outline the procedure for reconciling a checking or savings account register. Note that you cannot cancel the reconciliation process after you begin it.

Use Quicken to balance your checkbook.

1. Choose Select Account from the Main menu.

2. Select the checking account you want to reconcile.

3. Press F6 (*Activities*), and then select the Reconcile option. The Reconcile Register with Bank Statement window appears, showing the opening balance calculated from your previous reconciliation.

4. Enter the ending balance from your bank statement.

Before you begin the reconciliation process, you can print a report showing the transactions that were outstanding after you reconciled your statement last time. When the Reconcile Register with Bank Statement window appears, press F9 (*Print Last Recon Report*). Select which printer to use and whether to print a summary or full report (printing reconciliation reports is discussed in steps 9 through 13 in this section).

5. Enter any service charges and the category in which you record bank charges. If you want to keep service charges separate from check-printing or CheckFree-subscription charges, record the first charge in the Service Charge field now, and record other charges in the register later.

6. If this is a savings account or an interest-earning checking account, enter the amount of the interest and the category in which you record interest income.

Figure 11.1 shows an example of a completed bank account reconciliation screen.

After you complete the last field on the screen, the Reconciliation Summary screen appears. It lists the open transactions in your checking account register. If you made a service charge or interest entry, it is listed with an asterisk (*) in the Cleared column (labeled C) to indicate it is cleared.

7. Using your bank statement for reference, mark each check and deposit listed there as cleared in your register. To mark an item, press Return beside it.

The spacebar toggles between marking and unmarking items. You can also press F8 to enter the first and last numbers in a series of checks you want to mark cleared. However, you cannot unmark a range of items.

As you mark the items, the program totals the withdrawals and deposits that have been posted by your bank. These items are used

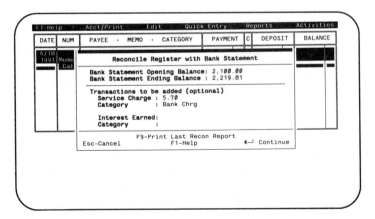

Figure 11.1: Entering bank statement information

to adjust the ending balance in your register to reconcile it with the new balance on your statement. The difference should be zero when you have completed the reconciliation.

8. After you've marked all the items, and the bank statement and your check register balance, the Difference field will contain 0.00. Press Ctrl-F10 to exit the reconciliation process.

In the example in Figure 11.2, the Reconciliation Summary screen indicates a $10.20 difference. When the account doesn't balance (there is an amount in the Difference field), you should stop and research the discrepancy. If you press Ctrl-F10 to signal you have completed the reconciliation before the account balances, Quicken warns you that there is a problem and lists possible reasons for the difference. The following section describes your alternatives when the account cannot be reconciled.

9. When the account does balance and you exit the reconciliation process, Quicken changes the asterisks in the Cleared column to Xs and asks if you want to print a reconciliation report. Respond N or Y. If you respond N, your bank account reconciliation is completed.

Print a reconciliation report for a record.

```
 F1-Help     Acct/Print      Edit      Quick Entry     Reports     Activities

  NUM    C   AMOUNT    DATE        PAYEE                      MEMO

              914.89   6/15/91 June 15th Pay Check
         *      -5.70   6/30/91 Service Charge
  1001   *    -450.00   6/ 1/91 Adobe Property Managem 6722 Pueblo Ave, June
  1002   *     -79.18   6/13/91 Southwest Bell         602-757-8726
  1003   *     -15.00   6/13/91 Mesa Water District    6722 Pueblo Ave
  1004        -100.00   6/17/91 VISA                   On Account
  1005   *     -35.00   6/17/91 Pete's Lawn Service    June Lawn Care
▶ 1006   *    -200.00   6/18/91 Alphabet Ranch         Sarah's Childcare

  ▮ To Mark Cleared Items, press Space Bar  ▮ To Add or Change Items, press F9

                         RECONCILIATION SUMMARY
         Items You Have Marked Cleared (*)
       ------------------------------------ Cleared (X,*) Balance   2,230.01
         6    Checks, Debits      -784.88   Bank Statement Balance  2,219.81
         1    Deposits, Credits    914.89   Difference                 10.20

  F1-Help          F8-Mark Range        F9-View as Register     Ctrl F10-Done
```

Figure 11.2: Reconciling a bank account

10. If you choose to print a report, select which printer to use.

11. If you want the date printed on the report to be different than the current date, enter another date in the Reconciliation Date field.

12. For the report title, enter a name that describes the range of activities included in this reconciliation, such as the range of dates or check numbers covered in the report (25 characters maximum).

13. Choose to print either a summary or full report. A full report includes totals and detail for both cleared and uncleared transactions. A summary report also shows totals for all transactions, but only includes detail for uncleared transactions.

The Print Reconciliation Report window remains on the screen after the report prints. You can print a summary report if you printed a detail report the first time, or vice versa.

When Your Account Doesn't Balance

Check your records if your account does not balance.

If a difference remains after you've marked all the cleared items, review your bank statement and account register. Press F9 to view the register. If you discover an error in your register, you can correct it. Perhaps you wrote a manual check and forgot to enter it in the register, or you recorded an amount that differs from the amount actually on the check. You might also need to record an automatic charge that doesn't qualify as a service charge.

When the register is displayed, you can add, edit, and delete transactions, as explained in Step 5. To return to the reconciliation process, press F9 again to view the list of transactions.

If you entered an incorrect ending balance, while the register is displayed, press F6 (*Activities*). Again, select the Reconcile option to redisplay the Reconcile Register with Bank Statement window, and then enter the correct ending balance. If you entered the service charge or the interest-earned amount incorrectly, you must edit those transactions in the register, not in the reconciliation window.

You can also force the balance by pressing Return and allowing Quicken to enter an adjustment in the register. The program prompts you to verify that you want to make the adjustment and allows you to enter a category to charge the adjustment against.

If you choose to exit the reconciliation process without balancing, press Esc. Quicken saves the work you have done. Your entries remain intact, the asterisk stays in the Cleared column (indicating the reconciliation process is incomplete), and the reconciliation attempt remains unbalanced. After you research the difference, begin the reconciliation process again and balance your account against your statement.

Reconciling Credit Card Accounts

Reconcile your credit card accounts to keep your Quicken records accurate.

When you receive your credit card statement, compare it with your credit card register to be certain you recorded every transaction. Follow these steps to reconcile the statement from the credit card company with your own entries in the credit card register:

1. Choose the Select Account option from the Main menu, and then select your credit card account from the account group list.

2. When the credit card register appears, press F6 (*Activities*).

3. Select the Pay Credit Card Bill option. (This is somewhat of a misnomer—you aren't actually paying the bill yet, although you can do so at the end of the reconciliation process.)

4. When the Credit Card Statement Information window appears, in the first field, enter the total of all charges and cash advances. Notice that finance charges are handled separately.

5. Enter the total of the payments you made and any credits posted to your account.

6. Be sure you enter the new, or *ending,* balance from the statement, not the beginning balance.

7. Enter the amount you were charged this month for finance charges and the category you use for interest paid. Figure 11.3 shows an example of a completed Credit Card Statement Information window.

The Reconciliation Summary window appears. The finance charge is already marked cleared, as indicated by the asterisk in the Cleared column.

8. Mark each charge and payment listed there as cleared in your register, using the techniques described earlier for marking checking or savings account items. The Difference field should contain zero when you have completed the reconciliation.

9. When your account balances, press Ctrl-F10 to exit.

If your account does not balance (there is an amount in the Difference field), you should review your credit card statement and register. As when you are reconciling bank accounts, you can press F9 to display the register and edit it as necessary. Press F9 again to return to the reconciliation process.

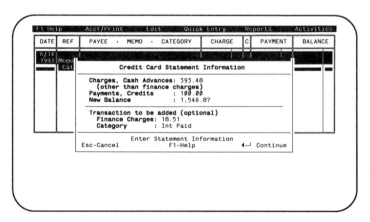

Figure 11.3: Entering credit card statement information

If you entered an incorrect amount in the Credit Card Statement Information window, press F6 (*Activities*), select Pay Credit Card Bill, and make the necessary changes when the window reappears. However, if you entered the finance charge incorrectly, you must change it in the register.

10. After your statement and account agree and you press Ctrl-F10, a window titled Make Credit Card Payment appears. If you do not want to make a payment now, press Esc. You will exit from the reconciliation process, and the items you marked will be cleared from the account.

11. If you want to make a payment, enter the bank account and indicate if you are issuing a handwritten check or not.

12. If the payment is not by handwritten check, the check window appears. The amount field shows the balance due on the credit card statement, and the credit card account is in the Category field. Enter another amount if you do not want to pay the balance in full.

13. If you are writing the check by hand, the checking account register appears, with the transaction for the credit card payment already entered for payment in full. You can complete the transaction with a check number, description, and memo. If you want to make a partial payment, enter the actual amount of the check in the Payment field.

Credit Card Register Adjustments

If you attempt to end the reconciliation process and an amount remains in the Difference field, Quicken displays a window titled Adjusting Register to Agree with Statement. The program creates an adjusting entry to force the balance in your register to agree with the credit card statement. The window notes the total amount of any payments or charges that the program assumes were not recorded in your register.

An adjusting entry forces the account to balance.

Be aware that the problem may be that you entered an incorrect total charges or total payments figure in the Credit Card Statement Information window. Double-check before making an arbitrary adjustment because it is best to locate the difference and record the missing transactions in the register instead.

Press Esc if you do not want to accept the adjustment calculated by the program. If you decide the adjustment is appropriate, you can either enter a category to charge the adjustment against or leave the adjustment uncategorized.

At any time, you can print a transaction summary report, which lists all transactions, cleared and not cleared, for a specific credit card account. Printing reports that restrict the information to a specific account is covered in Step 16.

Reconciling Investment Accounts

Investment account reconciliation is similar to checking and savings account reconciliation. After you select the account you want to reconcile, press F6 (*Activities*), and then choose Reconcile.

Quicken displays the Reconcile Mutual Fund Account or the Reconile Investment Account window, with the starting balance (which is the ending balance from your last reconciliation). Enter the ending balance from your statement. You can optionally enter the ending price if you want Quicken to update the market value of your investment. Enter the ending balance date from your statement. When the Reconciliation Summary screen appears, press the spacebar to mark items that appear on your statement. When all items are marked, press Ctrl-F10.

If the statement and your register do not agree, a message appears. If you want Quicken to enter an adjustment in your register to force it to balance with your statement, press Return. However, the prudent action is to press Esc to display the register. There are three ways to correct the reconciliation, depending on the error:

- You can edit, delete, or add transactions to the register to bring it into accord with the statement.

- You can change the flag in the Cleared column by pressing F9 to display the item list and using the spacebar to place or erase an asterisk.

- You can correct the amounts you entered from the statement by pressing F6 when the register is displayed, selecting Reconcile from the Activities menu, and overriding the figures you originally entered in the Reconcile Mutual Fund Account or Reconcile Investment Account window.

When you press Ctrl-F10 to exit from a mutual fund account reconciliation, and the statement and register agree, the Share Balance Reconciled window displays the number of ending shares, the price per share, and the market value. If you reconciled another type of investment account, the Cash Balance Reconciled window appears. From this window, you can press Return to update prices (Step 8 explains how to update prices). Be aware that pressing Esc from either of these windows does not cancel the reconciliation process. Your work has already been recorded.

Step 12

Transfers and Split Entries

15

If you are taking full advantage of Quicken, your transactions may affect several accounts and categories. This step explains how transfers work and how to split transactions among several categories.

Entering a Transfer

A *transfer* is a movement of funds between accounts. A transfer can be money coming into or going out of an account. For example, suppose that you make your credit card payment with money from your savings account. As you record the withdrawal in your savings account register, you would enter the name of the credit card account in the Category field to indicate where the money went. Quicken automatically makes an offsetting entry in the credit card account, and places the name of the savings account in the Category field of the credit card register.

Enter a transfer to move funds from one account to another.

To enter a transfer, complete the fields in the register or on the check as usual until you reach the Category field. In that field, enter the name of the offsetting account surrounded by brackets, such as [Credit Corp]. Alternatively, you can press Ctrl-C to display the category and transfer list, highlight the account receiving the transfer, and press Return.

Figures 12.1 and 12.2 illustrate the entries in a check register and a loan register that are the result of writing a check charged to a loan account. Quicken entered the check in the check register as always, and also made an offsetting entry for the transfer in the loan register.

If you delete a transaction that was involved in a transfer, the offsetting entry is also deleted. For example, if you void a check that was used to make a loan payment, the payment in the loan register is also deleted, and your loan balance will be adjusted accordingly.

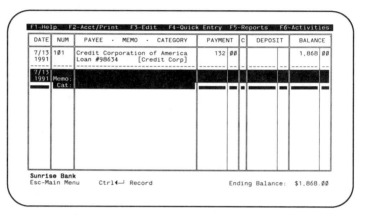

Figure12.1: The original check register entry

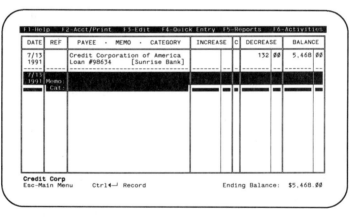

Figure 12.2: The offsetting loan register entry

Split transactions to charge them to multiple categories.

Splitting Transactions

A *split transaction* charges the amount to more than one category. For example, when the interest portion of a loan payment is tax-deductible, you may want to divide that transaction between principal and interest categories.

You can split a transaction while you are writing a check in Quicken or when you are recording a transaction in a register. To split a transaction, press Ctrl-S in the Category field. The Split Transaction window will appear. Enter the category, a description of the transaction, and the amount to charge to that category. For the amount to charge for the current category, the program supplies the entire amount remaining on the transaction. Override the default entry by entering the actual amount you want to charge. You can split a transaction among up to 30 categories.

In the example shown in Figure 12.3, a check for propane service is being split between the user's own home and her mother's adjoining cottage. Both parts of the transaction are charged to the category Utilities; however, a subcategory for the main house and the cottage (designated by house numbers) further defines each entry.

When the primary category is the same for both entries, as in Figure 12.3, you can use a shortcut for the second entry: press the quotation mark key (") in the Category field to copy the category from the first entry instead of retyping or reselecting it.

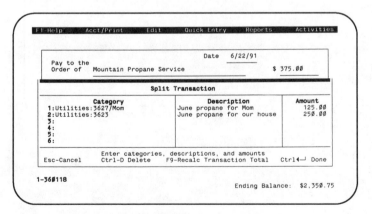

Figure 12.3: Splitting a transaction

The example in Figure 12.3 also shows that the portion charged for the cottage contains a class named Mom. This class designation makes it possible to print reports that list all activity pertaining to Mom, including utilities, clothing, or health insurance premiums. Filtering reports in this manner is discussed in Step 16.

When your entries are accurate, press F10 to record them. The check for the sample split transaction in Figure 12.3 is shown in Figure 12.4. The first category appears in the Category box, but the notation [SPLIT] at the bottom of the box indicates other entries exist for this check. If you want all the categories involved in a split transaction to be printed on your checks, you must use voucher-style checks.

If, when you begin the entry, you are uncertain how much the check should be written for, let Quicken calculate the total. Enter the payee, then press Ctrl-S to go directly to the Split Transaction screen, leaving the Amount field blank. As you enter the individual category amounts, Quicken increases (or decreases if you enter a minus figure) the amount of the check. Press F10 when you have entered all the line items, and then complete the Address and Memo fields for the check.

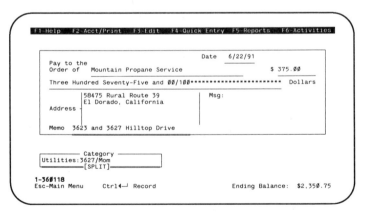

Figure 12.4: A check with a split transaction

Be aware that if you want to split a transaction, you cannot also record it as a transfer. You must make a separate entry in the off-setting register. For example, if you want to charge a check you are writing for a car payment to principal and late fee categories, you must make a separate entry in your loan account to show the payment.

Editing Split Transactions

You can edit a transaction that has been split among several cate-gories while you are entering it or after it is recorded. If you have already recorded the transaction, display it, and then press Ctrl-S to view its detail. Move the cursor to the field you want to change, press Ctrl-Backspace to delete the existing data, and enter the new data.

You can add or remove lines. To delete an entire line from the transaction, position the cursor on it and press Ctrl-D. Every change you make results in a new program-calculated remainder (either positive or negative depending on what is required to equal the original amount of the transaction) on the last line of the split.

You can easily modify the original amount of the transaction to match the changes you are making to the category. Delete the de-fault remainder that Quicken calculates, and then press F9 (*Recalc Transaction Total*). Quicken will sum the individual line items and change the transaction total to match the result.

Step 13

Recurring Transactions

Many of your financial activities are repetitive. You might make a house payment monthly, receive your paycheck semimonthly, and give your children an allowance each week. Instead of entering the entire transaction time and time again, you can save the original transaction and recall it as often as necessary. This step explains how to handle recurring transactions.

Setting Up Recurring Transactions

You can set up the checks you write regularly, as well as repetitive entries in a register, as recurring transactions.

Memorizing Checks

Quicken provides a function called *memorize,* which allows you to store a transaction and later copy it. For example, you can have Quicken memorize a check for monthly rent, so that you can recall the previously stored transaction each month instead of writing the check.

Quicken can memorize check information for recurring payments.

Follow these steps to set up a recurring check:

1. Choose Select Account from the Main menu, and then select the bank account to use.

2. When the register appears, press Ctrl-W to access the Write Checks function.

3. Complete the check form as usual, as explained in Step 9, but don't record the check.

4. After you complete the Category field, press F4 (*Quick Entry*) to display the memorizing options.

5. Select Memorize Transaction.

A shortcut is to bypass the Quick Entry menu by pressing Ctrl-M after completing the Category field.

6. The program highlights the fields in the check that will be memorized and prompts you to verify that you do want to memorize the transaction. Press Return to continue. If you want to cancel the request to store the transaction, press Esc.

7. After Quicken memorizes the transaction, you can either record it as a check awaiting printing, or delete it if you do not want to process the transaction at this time.

Memorizing Transactions

Recurring register entries can be memorized to save data-entry time.

Some of your recurring transactions may not involve writing a check. For example, your insurance company may be authorized to automatically deduct the monthly premium from your checking account, or your paycheck deposit may be the same amount each time. In these cases, the entry is made directly in the bank register.

The following steps outline the procedure for creating a recurring register entry.

1. Choose Select Account from the Main menu and select the account to use.

2. When the register appears, enter the transaction as usual and categorize it, but do not record it yet.

3. Press Ctrl-M to memorize the transaction, review the fields that will be memorized, and press Return to verify the action.

4. Record the transaction, or delete it if you do not want to process it now. The definition of the recurring transaction remains in the memorized transaction file.

Processing a Recurring Transaction

All memorized transactions are kept in one file. The transaction is not specific to one account. In other words, you can define a check for one bank account and recall it to use for another bank account. Logically, however, recurring transactions should affect the same account every time.

When you recall a memorized transaction, you can edit it for the current entry or record it without changes. Note that if you change the amount of a transaction that has been split, the amount of the change will be included in the split as an uncategorized entry. Press Ctrl-S to view the split information and make appropriate changes to coincide with the new transaction amount.

Recalling a Memorized Check

To recall a memorized check, when the blank check form appears, press Ctrl-T. This displays the memorized transactions list, as shown in Figure 13.1 (the numbers in the Grp column on this screen are explained in Step 14).

Highlight the check you want to recall and press Return. Quicken will enter the memorized information on the current check. You can change any field. For example, you might want to indicate which month's mortgage you are paying in the Memo field. Press F10 when you are ready to record the check. It will await printing with any other checks you are writing.

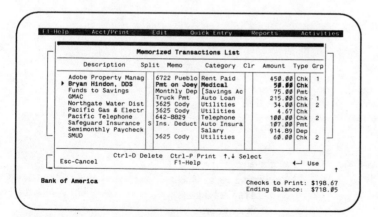

Figure 13.1: The memorized transactions list

Recalling Transactions in a Register

Recall a memorized transaction to fill in the register fields.

The transactions that Quicken has memorized can be recalled and placed in a register. Simply move the cursor to the first blank transaction field in the register and press Ctrl-T. When the memorized transaction list appears, select the transaction to recall. The fields in the register will be filled in with the stored definition. You can change the data in any field, or just press F10 to record the transaction. Any changes you make in the current transaction will not affect the stored definition.

You can place several recurring transactions in a *transaction group* and recall them for processing at one time. This step explains how to define and process transaction groups. Before you can create a transaction group, you must first create and memorize the transactions, as explained in Step 13.

Grouping Recurring Transactions

Any similar transactions that you process on a regular basis can be defined as a transaction group. For example, you may want to group your three loan payments that are all due on the first of each month, or your children's weekly allowances.

The following steps outline the procedure for creating a transaction group.

1. Select Register from the Main menu, and then press F4 (*Quick Entry*).

2. From the submenu, select Transaction Groups. A list of 12 possible groups appears, all with the notation <unused>.

You can bypass the Quick Entry menu by pressing Ctrl-J to access the transaction groups list.

3. Press Return to select the first unused group.

4. In the window that appears, at the first prompt

    `Name for this group:`

    enter a name that describes the type of transactions (20 characters maximum), such as *First of Month Bills* or *Utility Bills*.

5. At the prompt

    `In the Account to load before executing:`

Enter the transaction group frequency so Quicken will remind you to process the group.

enter the name of the account to which the transactions in this group pertain. You can press Ctrl-C to select the appropriate account.

You don't have to enter an account if the transactions are generic enough to be applicable to more than one account. Later, be sure to choose the account you want to affect before you select to execute the transaction group.

6. In the Frequency field, enter the number that corresponds to how often you want to process these transactions, as shown in the example in Figure 14.1.

When you start Quicken, if you have established frequency and dates for a transaction group, Quicken will display the reminder

Transaction group due

7. At the prompt

Next scheduled date:

Quicken supplies the current date. Override it to enter the first time you want to process this group. Thereafter, Quicken will calculate the date according to the frequency you entered.

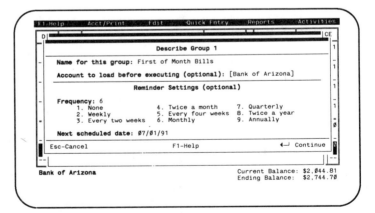

Figure 14.1: Creating a transaction group

Quicken does not automatically process a transaction group on the scheduled date. You must select to process them, as explained in the next section.

8. When you complete the fields in the window, the memorized transactions list appears. Move the cursor to the first transaction to include in the group and press the spacebar. The number of the group you are assigning the transaction to appears in the column titled Grp. You cannot assign a transaction to more than one group.

9. Continue to assign transactions to the group. Use the spacebar as a toggle to include or remove a transaction from the group. Remember to include only transactions that involve the same account.

10. After you finish assigning transactions to the group, press Return. The transaction group list will appear. It shows the group name, number of transactions, frequency, and next scheduled date.

11. Press Esc to exit from the transaction group function.

Editing Transaction Groups

To edit a transaction group, press Ctrl-J from the check format screen or account register. When the transaction group list appears, move the cursor to the group you want to change and press Ctrl-E. Change the heading information, or press F10 to move to the transaction listing. You can change the name, account to use, frequency, or scheduled date. You can also add memorized transactions to the group or remove them at any time. Use the spacebar to add or exclude transactions from the group. Press Return when you are finished making changes.

You can change the transaction group

Processing Transaction Groups

After you have defined a transaction group, you can process it at any time, regardless of the scheduled date.

Process the group at any time.

When you are ready to process the group, press Ctrl-J to access the transaction group listing. (If you did not assign an account to the group, be sure to choose the account you want to use before proceeding.) Move the cursor to the group you want to execute and press Return. At the prompt

```
Date of group:
```

enter the date you want the transactions recorded in the register. You can edit this date for individual transactions after they are recorded. Quicken displays a message indicating that the transactions are being recorded. The program also sets the next scheduled date according to the frequency you established. When the process is complete, press Return to return to the register or check format screen.

Checks that are included in the group are ready to print or transmit electronically (Step 17 discusses electronic payments).

Editing Recorded Group Transactions

You can change a recorded transaction.

After the transactions are recorded, Quicken allows you to edit them. You can begin from either the check format screen (if the transactions are checks) or the register screen (if the transactions are a mixture of checks and routine entries).

You can change the amount of the check before you disburse it. For example, you might have a group of checks set up for your water, garbage, electricity, gas, and telephone bills. The amounts may differ each month, but the payee, address, and category remain constant. You can process the checks as a transaction group, and then change the amounts to match this month's statements before you print them.

Quicken supplies many reports that provide information about your personal and business financial activities. Although you cannot actually design a report from scratch, you can specify the format and data to be included in the report. Customizing Quicken reports is discussed in Step 16. This step describes how to generate standard reports.

Types of Reports

When you choose Reports from the Main menu, Quicken presents a submenu of report types: Personal, Business, and Investment. Each of these options displays a submenu of reports for the selected category, as described in the following sections.

Main report types are personal, business, and investment.

Personal Reports

You can select from the following types of personal reports:

- Cash Flow: Lists monies received and expended in each category per month for all bank, cash, and credit card accounts.

- Monthly Budget: Compares actual expenditures with budgeted expenses in each category per month for all bank, cash, and credit card accounts.

- Itemized Categories: Lists transactions by category for all accounts.

- Tax Summary: Lists transactions for tax-related categories for all accounts.

- Net Worth: Summarizes balances in all your accounts as of the printing date.

Business Reports

Many of the reports designated for business can also be valuable when analyzing your personal transactions. Quicken provides the following standard business reports:

- P & L Statement: Lists income and expenses totaled by category per month for all accounts.

- Cash Flow: Lists monies received and expended in each category per month for all bank, cash, and credit card accounts. (This format is the same as the personal cash flow report.)

- A/P by Vendor: Lists unprinted checks by payee for all bank accounts.

- A/R by Customer: Lists balances due from each customer per month for all other asset accounts.

- Job/Project Report: Totals income and expenses by class per month for all accounts.

- Payroll Report: Totals income and expenses by payee, subtotaled by category for all categories identified as Payroll for all accounts.

- Balance Sheet: Summarizes balances in all your accounts as of the printing date. (This format is similar to the personal net worth report.)

Investment Reports

You can generate five different types of investment reports:

- Portfolio Value: Lists the value of your investments on a specific date—number of shares, most recent price, cost basis, and unrealized gain or loss and market value as of the specified date.

- Investment Performance: Summarizes the average annual total return on investments during a specific date range.

- Capital Gains: Lists the capital gains for securities sold in a specific date range. You can use the information on this report for the Schedule D income tax form.

- Investment Income: Lists interest and dividend income, as well as margin interest expense. You can use the information on this report for the Schedule B income tax form.

- Investment Transaction: Shows the effect of transactions in a specific date range on the cost basis or market value of investments and cash balance in accounts.

Entering Printing Parameters

When you select to process a report, you can enter a title for it or accept the default report name as the title. Enter the periods (a period is one month) or dates to be included on the report.

After you specify the parameters, the report is displayed on screen. You can then take one of the following actions:

- Store the report format (perhaps to print the report later) by pressing Ctrl-M.

- Print the report by pressing F8.

- Cancel the report by pressing Esc.

Viewing Reports on Screen

Figure 15.1 shows an example of a transaction report displayed in abbreviated form; that is, the information in some columns is truncated. To view the entire entry in a column, press F9 to expand the columns to full width. Press F9 again to return them to the abbreviated form. The printed report will have the same column-width settings as those that appear on the screen.

Review your report data on the screen.

When the report is too long or wide to fit on your screen all at once, you can use the following keys to view it:

- PgUp or PgDn: Scrolls one page up or down.

```
                        TRANSACTION REPORT
                      1/ 1/91 Through 6/21/91
All Accounts
6/21/91
 Date    Acct    Num   Description    Memo        Category        Clr   Amount

 5/28  1-36011          Opening Balance          [1-36011]         X    1,628.57
 6/10  1-36011          Monthly Master           [1744-8904-3834]       -100.00
 6/16  1-36011          ATM Withdrawal           [Cash on Hand]         -150.00
 6/21  1-36011          Deposit Paychec June 1 - 1 Salary               972.18
 5/25  1744-89          Opening Balance          [1744-8904-3834] X   -1,234.88
 6/10  1744-89          Mellon Bank Mas Monthly Pa [1-36011]       X     100.00
 6/14  1744-89          Festive Frills  Summer's P Gifts           X    -156.94
 6/14  1744-89          Nordstroms      Business S Clothing        X    -236.54
 6/14  1744-89          White Pelican R Father's D Dining                -98.00
 6/16  1744-89          Finance Charges          Int Paid          X     -18.51
 6/ 1  Cash on          Opening Balance          [Cash on Hand]          125.00
 6/16  Cash on          Lunches week en          Dining                  -27.88
 6/16  Cash on          Gasoline week e 174 miles Auto Fuel               -11.92
                                                                            ↑↓
All Accounts
Esc-Create report   Ctrl M-Memorize   F1-Help   F8-Print   F9-Full column width
```

Figure 15.1: A report displayed on the screen

- Up arrow or down arrow: Scrolls one row up or down.

- Right arrow or left arrow: Shifts one column right or left.

- Tab or Shift-Tab: Shifts one screen right or left.

- Home or End: Moves to the upper-right or lower-left corner of the screen.

Printing the Report

When you request to print a report, you can send it to the following destinations by entering the related option number:

1. Report printer

2. Alternate report printer

3. Check printer

4. Disk (ASCII file)

5. Disk (1-2-3 file)

Your printers are defined using the Printer Settings option on the Change Settings menu. Alternate report printer settings depend on the type of printer you have. Most allow compressed print. Some allow landscape presentations.

If you select to create a hard copy, have your printer ready. The report prints as soon as you select a destination.

After the report is sent to the printer, it reappears on the screen. You can press F8 (*Print*) again and send the report to a different destination, perhaps to save it on disk or to print a second copy to distribute or file.

Changing Printer Settings

When you select a printer from the list, Quicken sets the defaults for the fields described in Table 15.1. If necessary, you can override the defaults according to the settings noted in your printer manual.

Prompt	*Settings*
Print to	Indicate the port to which printer is attached. PRN, LPT1, LPT2, and LPT3 are parallel ports; COM1, COM2, and AUX are serial ports.
Indent	If you have a wide-carriage printer, you can indicate how many spaces from the left margin you want printing to begin.
Lines per page	Most paper is 11 inches long and prints 6 lines per inch (lpi), resulting in 66 lines per page. If you use a laser printer, try 60 lpi for reports and 63 lpi for checks.
Print pitch	You can set the printing on your checks to be either 10 cpi or 12 cpi, if your printer supports both pitches.

Table 15.1: Printer Setting Prompts

Prompt	Settings
Characters per line	If you are using 8½-inch paper, a 10-cpi pitch typically prints 80 characters per line. If you use 12 cpi, the setting should be 96; for 17 cpi (compressed print), the setting should be 132.
Pause between pages	If you use single sheets rather than continuous page forms, have Quicken pause between pages so you can insert the next sheet of paper.
Page-oriented	If your printer, particularly a laser printer, uses single sheets of paper, select Y for page-oriented.
Supports IBM graphics characters	Quicken can use IBM graphic characters instead of hyphens and equal signs to separate your heading from the data on a report if your printer supports those graphic characters.

Table 15.1: Printer Setting Prompts (continued)

If you need to reset the printer parameters before printing, press F9 (*Set Up Printer*), and then choose the printer setting you want to alter.

Quicken defines a *custom report* as one that includes only selected records. You can restrict reports by a date range or an account and select when and how to subtotal amounts. Once you set the parameters for a custom report, you can save the report format for future use.

Types of Custom Reports

In addition to the personal, business, and investment types of reports, Quicken provides the following reports, which are listed on the Custom Reports submenu:

- Transaction: Lists specific transactions according to your selection criteria.

- Summary: Lists all transactions for the specified categories, classes, payees, or accounts, according to your selection criteria.

- Budget: Compares actual income and expenses with the monthly budget, according to your transaction, account group, and subtotaling criteria.

- Account Balances: Lists balances of all accounts in the current account group, according to your transaction and date criteria.

You can also customize any of the personal, business, or investment reports provided by Quicken before printing them. Just press F8 (*Customize*) in the Report Title field, and then design the report as described in the following sections.

Customizing a Report

The report items that can be customized depend on the type of report. You may be able to define a date range, the fields you want included, how you want the data on the report subtotaled, and which accounts you want included in the report.

Row Heading

Row head-ings con-trol the report order.

The row heading determines how the report is sorted. In reports that offer row headings, you can select one from the following:

- Category
- Class
- Payee
- Account

Column Heading

Column headings control subtotal-ing.

The column heading, which is listed across the top of the page, controls the subtotals on the report. You can choose to subtotal your data for any type of custom report. Select one of the follow-ing column headings (the choices available vary according to the report you are customizing):

- None (don't subtotal)
- Week
- Two weeks
- Half month
- Month
- Quarter
- Half year
- Year
- Category
- Class

- Payee
- Account

Investment reports offer some other subtotaling options:

- Security
- Security type
- Investment goal
- Short-term versus long-term gains

Accounts to Include

You select which accounts you want included in the report by your response to the prompt

```
Use Current Account/Selected Accounts (C/A/S)
```

Include one, all, or selected accounts.

Enter C to include only the current account, A for all accounts in the current account group, or S to select accounts from the current account group. If you enter S, you can then press the spacebar to select (or unselect) accounts on the list.

Report Filters

A *filter* allows you to exclude data that does not meet your selection criteria from a report. You can filter reports by the data in the Payee, Memo, Category, and Class fields.

To filter a report, while the Create Report screen is displayed, press F9 (*Filter*). Then enter your selection criteria in the appropriate fields, as follows:

- If you leave the field blank, the transaction will be considered for inclusion regardless of the data found in that field.

- If you only want to include transactions that contain specific data in a field, enter the exact characters you want to match; for example, *Birthday*.

- To locate a string of characters regardless of where they appear in the field, precede and follow the characters with two dots. For example, if you search for *..mas..*, the program will find: *master*, *Christmas*, and *unmask*.

- To exclude a transaction that contains certain data in a field, place a tilde (~) in front of the keyword, or in front of the matching characters; for example, *~..mas..*, or *~Birthday*.

If you enter selection criteria for more than one field, a transaction will be included in the report only if it matches each set of criteria.

Filter reports to exclude or include data.

After you enter your selection criteria in the fields, respond to the six additional prompts to filter the report further. You can select categories to include from the list of categories, or classes to include from the list of classes. Respond Y at the appropriate prompt and complete the screen. When the list of categories or classes appears, use the spacebar as a toggle to mark the ones to include or exclude, and then press Return.

If you want to restrict the report to categories that are for tax purposes, respond Y to the prompt

```
Tax related categories only? (Y/N)
```

To restrict the report to transactions whose amounts meet certain selection criteria, enter the comparison and the value at the prompt

```
Below/Equal/Above:  the amount:
```

For example, you can include amounts that are below $100, equal to $30, or above $1,500.

Select which transactions to include at the prompt

```
Payments/Deposits/Unprinted Checks
```

Choose to print only payments, deposits, or unprinted checks. Enter A to include all three types of transactions.

If you want to filter reports by cleared status (as indicated by the Cleared column in the register), respond to the prompt

```
Cleared status is blank, *, X.
```

Enter a Y in the appropriate field if you want to include only those transactions that are not cleared (blank cleared status), pending (have an asterisk), or cleared (have an X). Step 5 explains the symbols in the account register's Cleared column.

You can press Ctrl-D to clear all the selection criteria and begin again.

Report Options

A *report option* is a means of controlling the presentation of the selected data on a report.

To choose report options, while the Create Report screen is displayed, press F8 (*Options*). Then respond to the following prompts (the prompts you will see depend on the type of report you are preparing).

At the prompt

```
Report organization
```

you can select to separate reports by income, expense, and transfer activity, or to print a cash-flow report format, which includes transfers among the income and expenses.

For a personal balance sheet or business net worth report, you can select either net worth or balance sheet as the report organization. Both formats list assets, liabilities, and the difference, but the balance sheet format also includes equity.

You can exclude or include transfers by your response to the prompt

Transfers

When you include all transfers, the report shows both the originating and offsetting transactions. Exclude transfers to eliminate both the originating and offsetting transactions involved in a transfer. Alternatively, you can select to include only transfers to accounts that are not included in the report.

For an investment report, you will see the prompt

Include unrealized gains (Y/N)

Enter Y to include the gains and losses resulting from price changes on investments.

To print a summary report, respond Y to the prompt

Show totals only (Y/N)

The report will include only totals, without supporting detail.

To show the amount charged to each category in a split transaction, enter Y at the prompt

Show split transaction detail (Y/N)

Split transactions are automatically included when you filter or subtotal by category or class.

Your response to the prompt

Show memo/category/both

determines whether the report includes a column for memos only, a column for categories only, or columns for both.

If you want to round amounts to whole dollars, enter N at the prompt.

Show cents when displaying amounts (Y/N)

Your response to the prompt

Normal/Suppressed/Reversed subcategory display

controls the inclusion of subcategories and subclasses. Select Suppressed if you do not want to see subcategories and subclasses. Select Reversed if you want to report by subcategory or subclass instead of sorting first by category.

Memorizing Reports

After you customize a report, you can have Quicken memorize it for future use. Report formats you have saved can be processed, renamed, or deleted.

Memorize reports that you want to reuse.

You can choose to have the report memorized from the Create Report screen (after you enter the report title and set up the filter and the report options) or while the processed report appears on the screen. Press Ctrl-M, and then enter a name for the report in the Title field. Use a name that will differentiate this report format from other memorized reports. You can establish and memorize various formats with their own selection parameters for the same Quicken report. All parameters except the date range are saved, and then the program redisplays the Create Report screen.

To work with a memorized report, select Memorized Reports from the Reports menu. On the memorized report list, move the cursor to the report and take one of the following actions:

- To make changes to the report, press Return. You can change the filter and options for a particular printing, but the memorized report format will not change.

- To delete a report format you no longer need, press Ctrl-D. This removes only the report format with the specific parameters you created, not the actual report.

- To rename a memorized report, press Ctrl-E. Then press Ctrl-Backspace to erase the existing name and enter the new one.

- To print the report, press Return twice to display the report on the screen, and then press F8.

To pay bills electronically, you need a product called CheckFree in addition to Quicken. You can order CheckFree through Intuit, the developers of Quicken, by completing the form that comes with your software (or contact the CheckFree Corporation in Columbus, Ohio directly).

You also need a Hayes-compatible modem. If you do not already have a modem, you can purchase one from CheckFree or another vendor.

Modem Settings

Your modem must be set properly in order to transmit data to the CheckFree Corporation. Quicken provides a screen where you can enter the modem settings.

To set your modem, follow these steps:

1. Select Change Settings from the Main menu, then Electronic Payments from the submenu.

2. Choose Modem Settings from the submenu to display the Electronic Payment Settings screen.

3. As the serial port to be used by the modem, indicate the communications port to which your modem is attached.

4. For modem speed, enter the baud rate your modem and the CheckFree Corporation support.

5. Indicate whether you have tone (push-button phone) or pulse (rotary phone) dialing.

6. For the number to dial for the CheckFree payment processing service, enter the telephone number supplied by the CheckFree Corporation, including the area code and any additional numbers necessary to obtain an outside line, such as 9.

7. When you are ready to use the Electronic Payment feature, enter Y at the prompt

   ```
   Turn on Electronic Payment capability:
   ```

   You can also enter custom modem settings. Quicken will send the additional information to the modem before attempting transmission. These codes should be noted in your modem manual. To enter other modem settings, press F8 *(Custom Modem Initialization)* from the Electronic Payment Settings screen and type the codes in the Codes field.

Setting Up Accounts for Payments

First au-
thorize
CheckFree
to make
payments.

You can make electronic payments from any checking or savings account you have established in Quicken. You must first, however, authorize CheckFree to withdraw funds from the account. The authorization form is included when you sign up with CheckFree.

Follow the steps below to set up your bank accounts for transmission to CheckFree:

1. Select Change Settings from the Main menu, then Electronic Payment from the submenu.

2. Select Account Settings to display the Set Up Account for Electronic Payments screen, which lists your established bank accounts.

3. Place the cursor on the account you want to set up and press Return.

4. At the prompt

   ```
   Set up for electronic payment (Y/N):
   ```

   enter Y. The Electronic Payment Account Settings screen appears.

5. Enter your first name, middle initial, and last name in the appropriate fields.

6. Enter your street address on the two lines provided, followed by the city, state, zip code, and home phone number in the designated fields.

7. In the Social Security Number field, enter your CheckFree identification number. If you are using only one bank account for CheckFree payments, this is your social security number. If you are transmitting payments from more than one bank account, use the number designated by CheckFree for the account you are setting up. You cannot enter the same number for two accounts.

8. In the last field, enter the identification number assigned to you by CheckFree for this bank account.

When you complete the last field, the Set Up Account for Electronic Payment screen reappears. The notation Enabled appears beside the account you set up. You can continue to set up other bank accounts for electronic submissions or press Esc to exit. In your account listing, the Type field for this bank account will contain a small triangle to indicate that the account has been set up for electronic payments.

Setting Up Electronic Payees

Before you can send electronic payments, you must set up electronic payees.

Follow these steps to set up an electronic payee:

1. From either the bank register or the check format screen, press Ctrl-Y to display the electronic payee list.

2. Press Return in the Set Up a New Payee field.

3. Enter the payee name (maximum of 28 characters).

4. Enter the street address, city, state, and zip code in the provided fields. CheckFree may need this address to mail your payment to the payee, so be sure it is correct.

Enter payee information before making payments.

5. Enter the payee's area code and phone number. Again, CheckFree might use this information to contact the payee, so verify that your entry is correct.

6. Enter the account number assigned to you by the payee, such as your credit card or loan number. This is the information the payee will use to credit your account with the payment.

If you are preparing checks and enter a payee you have not previously set up, Quicken displays the message

`Electronic Payee Not Found`

and gives you the option of adding it during check entry.

Press Return to add the payee you have entered on the check, and then supply the information, as described above.

Duplicate Payees

If you have more than one account with the same payee, you must create an identifier for the payee name to distinguish each account from the original. For example, if you have two loans from your credit union—one for a car and another for a computer—you could identify them as *car* and *cmptr.*

When you enter the name of a payee that already exists, after you complete the address, phone number, and account number fields, Quicken displays a window with the prompt

`Additional identifying information required:`

Enter an identifier of up to ten characters to distinguish this payee from the original one. However, if you have used *all* 28 characters in the Name field, the identifier must be only a single character, such as *a* for auto and *c* for computer.

Quicken puts brackets around the identifier and does not transmit that information (nor print it if you issue a computer-generated check when making payments).

You can change or delete payee information, as long as there are no transmissions pending for that payee. To edit the information, display the electronic payee list, select the payee, and press Ctrl-E. To remove a payee entirely, select it from the list, press Ctrl-D, and verify the deletion.

Your changes and deletions will be sent to CheckFree with your next transmission.

Your payee changes are transmitted to CheckFree.

Writing Checks for Transmission

When you set up a bank account for electronic payments, you can still write computer-generated checks on that account. On the check form screen, use the F9 key to toggle between paper checks and electronic payments. Figure 17.1 shows the notation that appears above the memo line when the checks are set for electronic payments.

The name of the bank account appears in the lower-left corner of the screen. The dollar amount of checks pending transmission appears in the Check to Xmit field (checks that were prepared as paper checks are not included in this figure).

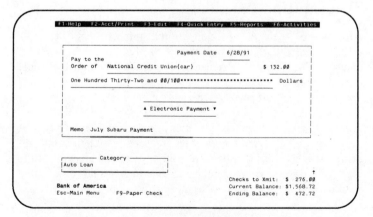

Figure 17.1: The electronic payment check format

The Current Balance field amount is what the balance is as of the current date, without deducting any postdated checks. The Ending Balance field shows what is in the account after all pending checks, electronic and paper, have been deducted.

In Figure 17.1, the payee's name is followed by an identifier in brackets to indicate that there is more than one account with this payee. As explained earlier, the payee will not see the identifier.

When you write an electronic payment, the check date automatically defaults to five days in the future to allow time for transmission and processing. You can enter a later date, but not an earlier one. Complete the check format by entering the payee's name, the amount of the payment, and optionally a memo and a category. Writing checks is covered in more detail in Step 9.

The checks to print and the checks to transmit are stored separately. The list of pending checks includes either paper checks or electronic payments, depending on the F9 toggle setting. The amount of paper checks to print will appear in the Checks to Print field when you press F9 to toggle to the paper checks written on the same account.

Transmitting Payments

After you write the checks, you can transmit payments electronically. Access the transmission screen by pressing F2 (*Acct/Print*) and selecting Transmit Payments. The transmission will include only the checks written on the current account. You must change accounts to transmit checks written on another bank account.

Preview your payments before sending them.

After selecting to transmit, you can preview what is about to be sent. Press F9 (*Preview*) to view the transactions. The list that appears includes checks to be sent, new payees, and changes to the electronic payee list. Your edits and deletions are not transmitted until all pending transactions for those payees have been sent.

If you notice an error, press Esc to exit from the transmission function. To begin the transmission, press Return. Quicken will initialize your modem and display messages as the transmission progresses. CheckFree returns a confirmation number to Quicken for each transmission. You can use this confirmation number to identify stop payments or inquiries, as discussed in the following sections.

Be aware that all your payees may not be able to accept electronic submissions. When this is the case, CheckFree prints a paper check from the data you transmitted and mails it to the payee. This is why the payee address and phone number in the payee record are so important. To avoid late charges, consider the extra time it may take for postal delivery.

Stopping Payment on Transmitted Checks

Just as you would go to a bank and complete forms to stop payment on a paper check, you transmit information to CheckFree in order to stop payment on an electronic check.

You can tell CheckFree to stop payment.

To stop payment on a check that you already transmitted to CheckFree, access the account register and highlight the check (finding transactions is discussed in Step 5). Press F3 (*Edit*) and select Transmit Stop Payment Request. (This option is available only when the bank account is set up as an electronic transfer account.) Respond Y when asked if you want to stop payment. Quicken transmits the stop payment request immediately. When the transmission is complete, Quicken places the confirmation number in the Memo field of the check and marks it void.

If the date on the check is earlier than the current date, you may not be able to stop payment. If, due to timing, the software will not allow you to send a stop payment, you can try calling CheckFree directly.

Sending Inquiries to CheckFree

On occasion, you may want to know the status of a check you transmitted to CheckFree. Such inquiries can be transmitted electronically.

To inquire about a payment that you previously transmitted to CheckFree, follow these steps:

1. Access the register for the check and highlight the payment in question.

2. Press F3 (*Edit*) and select Electronic Payment Inquiry.

3. Respond Y when asked if you want to send an inquiry.

4. When the Transmit Inquiry to CheckFree window appears, enter up to three lines of text.

5. When you are ready to transmit your inquiry, press Ctrl-Return. Quicken transmits the inquiry immediately.

You can also send an inquiry that does not pertain to a previously transmitted payment. To do so, press F6 (*Activities*) while writing checks or reviewing the register, and then select Send Electronic Mail to display the Transmit Inquiry to CheckFree window.

Step 18

Using Budgets

15

A *budget* is a preset amount you expect to receive or spend for a specific category. Everyone talks about staying within or going over their budget, but usually they are referring to figures they keep in their heads. Quicken's budgeting feature provides a more accurate measure of your spending habits.

A budget is not specific to one account type or account. Budgets cross account types, the same as categories do. In other words, you cannot establish a budget that covers only your credit card accounts, nor can you establish a budget just for your spouse's checking account. You can, however, restrict your reports to a comparison of the entire budget to the actual activity in just one account, as explained later.

Establish budgets for categories.

Setting Up Budgets

You can set up spending guidelines for each category you have established; however, you cannot create a budget for a subcategory or class. You can project the amount that you expect to receive, as well as the amount you expect to spend.

For some categories, such as clothing, you might want to spread your budget evenly across the entire year. For others, you might allot most of your expenditures to certain months. For example, your budget for the gift category might be assigned to holiday or birthday months.

The following steps outline the procedure for establishing an annual budget for a category:

1. Select Reports from the Main menu, then Personal Reports, then Monthly Budget. The Monthly Budget Report window will appear.

2. Press F7 (*Edit Budget Amounts*) to enter or edit a budget amount.

3. When the list of categories appears, move the cursor to the category you want to budget. If you want to enter a specific amount for each month, skip to step 6 in this section.

4. If the amount is the same each month, enter it in the Budget Amount field as your monthly allowance. Quicken will duplicate your entry in each of the 12 budget fields, including months already passed.

5. If you do not want to budget previous months, press Ctrl-E to display the monthly detail. Place the cursor in a previous month and press Ctrl-Backspace to erase the entry. Then skip to step 8 in this section.

6. When the list of months appears, move the cursor to the first month you want to budget and enter the amount for that month. You can use the Ins and Del keys to make corrections to your entry.

7. Continue adding unique budget amounts to the appropriate months. Figure 18.1 shows an example of various budget amount entries.

8. Press F10 to save your entries. Do not press Esc or your entries will be canceled.

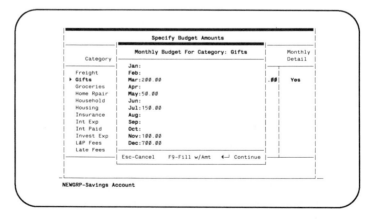

Figure 18.1: Entering varying budget amounts

If you want to budget the same amount for a group of months, you can have Quicken automatically fill in the amount. Place the cursor on the last month you completed and press F9 (*Fill*). The remaining months of the year will be filled in with the same amount.

You can also use the fill feature to clear the months below if the cursor rests on a blank amount. Any month left blank in a category that has been budgeted will show a budget of zero on reports. If you purchase a gift in a month with a budget of zero, a report will indicate that you are over your budget for that month.

Use the fill feature to copy or clear monthly budgets.

The Specify Budget Amounts screen displays the amount budgeted for the current month. If you entered varying amounts for other months, the notation Yes will appear in the Monthly Detail column. If you want a category to appear on budget reports, but do not want to enter a monthly budget, enter a zero in the Budget Amount field on the Specify Budget Amounts screen.

You can change the budget amounts for any month at any time. The new figure overrides the old one and will be used in future reports.

Printing Budget Reports

Budget reports list only the categories for which you have established a budget. They include the amount you actually spent, the amount of your budget, and the difference. Income and expense categories, labeled Inflows and Outflows, respectively, are listed and totaled separately.

You can compare the budget amount against one, several, or all your accounts. For example, perhaps you record clothing purchases in your bank account, your cash account, and your credit card account. The clothing category amount will include amounts from all three accounts. The clothing budget remains constant, but you can compare the budgeted amount with the combined expenditures recorded in just the bank and credit card accounts. In this

Compare budget amounts with one or more accounts.

case, clothes bought with pocket money are not considered in the actual-to-budget comparison.

Personal Monthly Budget Report

To print the Monthly Budget Report, select Reports from the Main menu, then Personal Reports, then Monthly Budget. The default report format includes subtotals by month for only the first account in your bank account list. Enter the range of months you want on the report, and, optionally, a title. You can change the subtotal column headings and the accounts to include by pressing F8 (*Customize*) and setting up the custom report (see Step 16 for details).

Custom Budget Report

To generate a custom budget report, select Reports from the Main menu, then Custom Budget Report. You can enter a title, subtotal preference, dates to include, and select accounts to use.

A subtotal selection of None totals all months in the date range together. If you select other subtotal options, Quicken accumulates or divides the monthly budget amounts according to your column headings. For example, if you request a quarterly report, Quicken adds the January, February, and March amounts together for the first budget-to-actual comparison.

If you select a period of less than one month, Quicken performs some intricate calculations. To report on one-half month, Quicken divides the monthly budget by the number of days in the month to arrive at a daily amount specific to that month. For example, a $100 budget for February would be divided by 28 for a $3.571 daily budget.

The first half of the month is considered to be the first to the fifteenth. The second half of the month is the remaining days. The number of days is multiplied by the daily budget. Thus, a budget of 100 on a report with increments of one-half month for February would show 2/1–2/15 as the first half month, with $53.57 as the budget. The second half month would be 2/16–2/28, with a budget of $46.42.

As with any custom report, you can filter and memorize the format. Press F9 (*Filter*) to restrict the report criteria beyond the subtotal, date, and account specifications. From the custom formatting screen, press Ctrl-M to memorize the format.

Memorize or filter your budget reports.

Activity from a business operation should be handled in a distinct account group set up for that purpose. You should also set up categories specific to your business; do not assign personal and business transactions to the same categories.

Bookkeeping Methods

Businesses can keep their books on either a cash or an accrual basis. With the *cash-basis method,* you record income when you receive money and expenses when you write a check. *Accrual bookkeeping* means recording income when you make the sale, regardless of when you will be paid, and recording an expense when you obligate yourself, regardless of when you will tender payment.

Quicken works best for a cash-basis business that is service-oriented. You cannot adequately keep track of your inventory with Quicken. Also, Quicken's form of accrual bookkeeping does not follow traditional, comprehensive accounting practice. Typically, you will use Quicken for your business if your finances are not complex or you can legally operate on a cash basis.

The government has rules on how a set of business books must be handled. You should consult an accountant on the appropriate way to record transactions for your business.

Assets in Business

The assets you maintain for a business are typically stock you keep on hand for resale, receivables, and equipment. Quicken maintains the asset, Cash, in a bank or cash account.

Record your business assets.

In a cash-basis system, when you buy a computer, for example, you can write off the equipment purchase when you make it, as long as it falls under a certain dollar amount. You would write a check to the vendor, enter the appropriate expense in the Category field (Equipment), and be done with it.

If you want to keep track of each asset individually, you need to set up an asset account for each piece of equipment. Then you would enter an increase to the asset account (Equipment) and a decrease to another account (Cash). In Quicken, this is accomplished by entering a transaction in the originating register, the one for your checking account. In the Category field, you would enter the name of the appropriate equipment account, and Quicken would make a transfer entry (Step 12 describes transfers).

When the price of the equipment you purchase is more than a certain dollar amount, tax law requires that you record its depreciation over a specified period of time. *Depreciation* is a paper expense that reduces the value of an asset. Periodically, you would enter a decreasing transaction in the asset register and charge the expense category, Depreciation. Usually, you will record depreciation monthly, but it can be done yearly if you do not need timely financial statements.

Accounts receivable are a special type of asset.

Money your customers owe you is a unique type of asset, called *accounts receivable.* To keep accrual books in Quicken, you must create an asset account for each customer and enter the full receivable amount as an increase to that account. Enter the appropriate income type (such as Sales or Repairs) in the Category field. Accounts receivable appear on your balance sheet as an asset.

For example, suppose that you allow a customer to pay for his car repair in installments. You would enter a transaction in the register for the customer to increase the balance in that asset account. In the Category field, enter the appropriate income category (Labor). When the customer makes a payment, enter the amount as a deposit in your checking account register, and in the Category field, enter the name of the customer's account. Quicken will make a transfer entry that reduces the account receivable. (You previously recorded the income when the customer made the purchase.)

In a cash-basis system, there are no true receivables. When the customer makes a payment, you simply enter the name of the income category in the Category field when you record the amount in your checking account register. There is no record of the sale or the income prior to receipt of the payment. On your balance sheet, there is no record of the amount owed to you.

Liabilities in Business

The liabilities you incur for a business are typically loans you received to start the business or buy equipment, and your debts to vendors. Large amounts you owe over a long period are usually called *notes payable*. Smaller, revolving amounts you owe to vendors are usually called *accounts payable*.

Keep track of your business debts.

To keep accrual books in Quicken, create a liability account for each debt, and enter the full amount you owe as an increase to that account. Notes and accounts payable appear on your balance sheet as liabilities.

For example, when you buy computer paper on credit, you would enter a transaction in the register for the vendor to increase the balance in that liability account. In the Category field, enter the appropriate expense category (Office Expense). To make a payment, write a check as usual, but in the Category field, enter the name of the vendor's account. Quicken will make a transfer entry that reduces that liability. (You recorded the expense when you bought the item.)

In a cash-basis system, there are no true liabilities. When you make a payment, you simply enter the name of the expense category in the Category field. Prior to writing the check, there is no record of the debt or the expense. Your balance sheet will not show the amount you owe.

The A/P by Vendor Report

Quicken's A/P by Vendor report is not a true picture of what is traditionally considered accounts payable. This report lists only amounts for which you have written, but not printed, a check.

For example, you might owe $4,000 on a business loan. When you write a check for your monthly loan payment of $150, the $150 will appear on the report, but not the remaining $3,850 balance. If you have printed the check, the amount will not appear on the A/P by Vendor report at all. Thus, you should not view this report as a statement of your liabilities.

The other business reports provided by Quicken are discussed in Steps 15 and 16.

Income and Expense Categories

Use categories to identify your business cash flow.

You probably want to identify each of the various ways money comes into and goes out of your business. This allows you to analyze where you generate the most profit and where you are spending the most money.

For example, a single category, Sales, would be sufficient to track income. However, categories titled Labor, Parts, and Rentals are more specific.

You could have a single category called Expenses, but you would get a better picture if you had expense categories titled Labor Costs, Parts Costs, and Rental Costs to compare with the related income categories. By subtracting what goes out from what comes in, you could determine the profit on each item. You could even divide categories for parts into Tires, Oil, and Air Filters.

Payroll Processing

To do payroll processing in Quicken, you must set up several accounts. Consider the requirements. You have the gross amount the employee earns. From that amount, you must subtract taxes and maybe union dues or insurance premiums. The amounts you withhold from an employee must be paid to someone else. You are just the temporary custodian of those funds. These amounts are recorded as liabilities. When you pay the taxes to the government, the dues to the union, or the premiums to the insurance company, you reduce your debts to those organizations.

Two terms that are useful to understand are deductions and contributions. *Deductions* are amounts that you take out of the employee's gross earnings. *Contributions* are amounts you, the employer, must pay in addition to anything the employee has withheld. For example, federal withholding tax is a deduction. The employee is the only one who pays it. If the company, not the employee, pays for health insurance, that is a contribution. Deductions are a liability only. Contributions are first an expense, but also a liability because you owe money to some other entity.

Income tax deductions are *not* expenses. However, the portion of income tax you, the businessman, must pay, such as social security or federal unemployment, *is* an expense. It is over and above the portion you withhold from the employee's wages. Gross wages, on the other hand, are an expense. That is the amount you pay to have the employee work for you.

To keep track of payroll activity, you need expense categories and liability accounts. Quicken requires that you begin each payroll-related category or account with the word *Payroll*. This allows the program to find the transactions for the payroll report (on the Business Reports submenu).

Set up expense categories and liability accounts for payroll activity.

You will need an expense category for two items:

- Gross wages
- FICA, employer's portion

You may need an expense category for other payroll expenses. If you, the employer, must pay all or a portion of something over and above what is deducted from your employees' gross wages, then set up a category. Here are some examples of other categories:

- State disability
- Workers compensation

- Federal unemployment
- State unemployment
- Retirement fund contributions

You will need a liability account for three items:

- Money withheld for federal income tax
- Amounts withheld for state income tax
- Amounts withheld and contributions for FICA

Additionally, you must set up a liability account for any other monies you withhold or must pay directly, such as the following:

- Union dues
- 401K
- 125P cafeteria plans
- Insurance premiums
- State disability
- Workers compensation
- Federal unemployment
- State unemployment
- Retirement fund contributions

These lists are not comprehensive. You should consult your accountant and know the government regulations that pertain to your payroll.

Split a payroll check transaction.

When you write a payroll check, enter the employee as the payee and the net wage after deductions as the payment amount. Then select to split the transaction.

The first entry in the Split Transaction window is the gross amount earned by the employee. Charge the full amount to the

Gross Payroll Expense category. Next, enter the federal withholding amount as a negative entry to the Federal Income Tax liability account. The third entry should be a negative amount for the state withholding amount, charged to the State Income Tax liability account.

Next, enter the amount withheld for FICA for the *employee's* portion as a negative entry charged to the FICA Tax liability account. Enter the *employer's* portion of FICA as a positive amount assigned to the FICA Expense category, and also make a negative entry for the same amount charged to the FICA Tax liability account. (See Step 12 for more information about transfers.)

Continue recording all other deductions and contributions. Remember, contributions require both a positive entry to an expense category and a negative entry to a liability account. Deductions from the employee's gross wages are simply positive entries to an expense category.

When you write a check for your quarterly tax payments to the government, in the Category field, enter the name of the Federal Income Tax liability account. Quicken will make a transfer entry that reduces that liability. Do the same thing for amounts due to any other institution. For example, enter the amount you owe the union or the insurance company, with the name of the Union Dues or Insurance Premium liability account in the Category field.

In his book, *Understanding Quicken 4,* Steve Cummings presents several good ideas and helpful references for using Quicken in a business.

Step 20

Exchanging Data

You exchange data between Quicken and other files via the export and import function. To *export* data is to copy information and place it into a file external to the current program. To *import* data is to bring external data into the current program.

Exporting Data

In Quicken, you can export data from the current register to an ASCII file. You can then use the information in a spreadsheet or word processing program.

Follow these steps to export Quicken data:

1. Select the register of the account from which you want to export data.

2. Press F2 (*Acct/Print*), and then select Export from the submenu.

3. Enter the name of the file to which you want to send data, including the drive and directory if it differs from the current drive and directory. Use DOS file-naming conventions. Quicken does not assign an extension to the file name.

4. Enter the beginning and ending dates of the transactions you want to export.

Export Quicken data that you want to use in other programs.

The file will be created as soon as you enter these dates. Quicken will warn you if you already have a file of the same name. You can press Return to overwrite the existing file, or press Esc to cancel the process and enter a different file name.

The exported file takes on the Quicken Interchange Format (QIF). The file begins with a header indicating the type of account from which the data was drawn. Each item is preceded by the identifying letter (listed later in this step), and the entire transaction ends with a caret symbol (^).

Importing Data

Quicken also allows you to import data from an ASCII or CheckFree file. ASCII files must be in the import format Quicken recognizes, QIF. You would only import data from a CheckFree file if you had been using CheckFree software before you began to use Quicken.

If you have been using another software product to track your check writing, you could use the import function to move that data into Quicken. However, you must first convert the previous data into an ASCII file, and then enter the QIF parameters before Quicken can accept the data. You might find it easier to just reenter the transactions in Quicken.

Import files to merge accounts or move transactions.

A more common use of the import function is to merge existing Quicken accounts into one, or to move transactions from one register to another. You must first export the data from the individual accounts into distinct files, and then import each file into the new consolidated account.

Account File Structure

Quicken accepts only files with a QIF structure.

Quicken will only accept data from an ASCII file if it is in the proper format. Investment accounts are treated differently from the other five Quicken account types.

To set up a QIF file for a noninvestment account, enter each transaction on a separate line and place the ^ symbol at the end of each transaction.

You can optionally place a header related to the type of Quicken account to which you are sending data. Here are some examples:

```
!Type:Bank
!Type:Cash
!Type:CCard
!Type:Oth A
!Type:Oth L
```

Begin each item in the transaction with one of the following letters, as appropriate to the field it should occupy in a Quicken register:

D   Date

N   Number

P   Payee

M   Memo

L   Category or transfer/class

T   Amount

C   Cleared status

S   Category or class in each entry of a split transaction

E   Description in each entry of a split transaction

$ Amount in each entry of a split transaction

A   Address (five lines maximum)

Investment Account File Structure

As for noninvestment account files, a QIF file for an investment account has each transaction on a separate line and a ^ symbol at the end of each transaction. However, you must begin an investment register import with the following header line:

```
!Type:Invst
```

Begin each item in the transaction with one of the following letters, as appropriate to the field it should occupy in an investment register:

D   Date

N   Action

Y   Security

I   Price

Q   Quantity of shares or split ratio

T   Amount

L   Account

C   Cleared status

M   Memo

O   Commission

Z   Type

P   Payee

N   Check number

The order in which the items are listed in the file within a transaction does not matter. If an item is not in the file, the corresponding field in the register will be blank.

Importing Data from an ASCII File

To import data from an ASCII file into Quicken, follow these steps:

1. Select the register into which you want to move the data.

2. Press F2 (*Acct/Print*) and select Import from the submenu.

3. In the File field, enter the name of the ASCII file. Remember, it must be in QIF structure.

4. Accept the default N at the prompt

    ```
    Special handling for transfers (Y/N):
    ```

    Enter Y to prevent duplicating transfers only if you are consolidating files that you exported from several Quicken accounts into one account.

5. Quicken will import the data and notify you when the process is complete. Press Return to review the transactions that were imported into the register.

After you have brought the transactions into the program, you can edit them as you would any other Quicken transactions.

If you are consolidating or moving transactions from one account to another, be aware that the original transactions are not automatically changed or deleted. You must delete the original transactions, or you will have the same entry in two accounts.

Importing Data from CheckFree

If you have been using CheckFree software to make electronic payments and now want to write and transmit payments to CheckFree through Quicken, you should update your Quicken register first, as follows:

1. Select the register you will be using in Quicken to transmit electronic payments.

2. Press F2 (*Acct/Print*) and choose Import from the submenu.

3. Enter the name of the drive and directory (usually CF) where your CheckFree program resides.

4. At the prompt

   ```
   Special handling for transfers (Y/N):
   ```

   enter Y to include transactions that are transfers. The transactions are displayed on the screen as they are imported.

If Quicken encounters a category you have not yet set up, it will allow you to add that category during the import process. If you press Esc to cancel the import process, the transactions that have been recorded will remain in your Quicken register. You can begin importing the file again, but remember to start with the day after the last transaction you already imported.

You cannot use both CheckFree and Quicken to make electronic payments. You must choose one or the other and use it consistently.

Index

Selections from The SYBEX Library

SPREADSHEETS AND INTEGRATED SOFTWARE

1-2-3 for Scientists and Engineers
William J. Orvis
341pp. Ref. 407-0

Fast, elegant solutions to common problems in science and engineering, using Lotus 1-2-3. Tables and plotting, curve fitting, statistics, derivatives, integrals and differentials, solving systems of equations, and more.

The ABC's of 1-2-3 (Second Edition)
Chris Gilbert
Laurie Williams
245pp. Ref. 355-4

Online Today recommends it as "an easy and comfortable way to get started with the program." An essential tutorial for novices, it will remain on your desk as a valuable source of ongoing reference and support. For Release 2.

The ABC's of 1-2-3 Release 2.2
Chris Gilbert
Laurie Williams
340pp. Ref. 623-5

New Lotus 1-2-3 users delight in this book's step-by-step approach to building trouble-free spreadsheets, displaying graphs, and efficiently building databases. The authors cover the ins and outs of the latest version including easier calculations, file linking, and better graphic presentation.

The ABC's of 1-2-3 Release 3
Judd Robbins
290pp. Ref. 519-0

The ideal book for beginners who are new to Lotus or new to Release 3. This step-by-step approach to the 1-2-3 spreadsheet software gets the reader up and running with spreadsheet, database, graphics, and macro functions.

The ABC's of Excel on the IBM PC
Douglas Hergert
326pp. Ref. 567-0

This book is a brisk and friendly introduction to the most important features of Microsoft Excel for PC's. This beginner's book discusses worksheets, charts, database operations, and macros, all with hands-on examples. Written for all versions through Version 2.

The ABC's of Quattro
Alan Simpson
Douglas J. Wolf
286pp. Ref. 560-3

Especially for users new to spreadsheets, this is an introduction to the basic concepts and a guide to instant productivity through editing and using spreadsheet formulas and functions. Includes how to print out graphs and data for presentation. For Quattro 1.1.

The Complete Lotus 1-2-3 Release 2.2 Handbook
Greg Harvey
750pp. Ref. 625-1

This comprehensive handbook discusses every 1-2-3 operating with clear instructions and practical tips. This volume especially emphasizes the new improved graphics, high-speed recalculation techniques, and spreadsheet linking available with Release 2.2.

The Complete Lotus 1-2-3 Release 3 Handbook
Greg Harvey
700pp. Ref. 600-6

Everything you ever wanted to know about 1-2-3 is in this definitive handbook. As a Release 3 guide, it features the design and use of 3D worksheets, and improved graphics, along with using Lotus under DOS or OS/2. Problems, exercises, and helpful insights are included.

Lotus 1-2-3 Desktop Companion
SYBEX Ready Reference Series
Greg Harvey
976pp. Ref. 501-8

A full-time consultant, right on your desk. Hundreds of self-contained entries cover every 1-2-3 feature, organized by topic, indexed and cross-referenced, and supplemented by tips, macros and working examples. For Release 2.

Lotus 1-2-3 Instant Reference
Release 2.2
SYBEX Prompter Series
Greg Harvey
Kay Yarborough Nelson
254pp. Ref. 635-9, 4 ¾" × 8"

The reader gets quick and easy access to any operation in 1-2-3 Version 2.2 in this handy pocket-sized encyclopedia. Organized by menu function, each command and function has a summary description, the exact key sequence, and a discussion of the options.

Lotus 1-2-3 Tips and Tricks
(2nd edition)
Gene Weisskopf
425pp. Ref. 668-5

This outstanding collection of tips, shortcuts and cautions for longtime Lotus users is in an expanded new edition covering Release 2.2. Topics include macros, range names, spreadsheet design, hardware and operating system tips, data analysis, printing, data interchange, applications development, and more.

Mastering 1-2-3
(Second Edition)
Carolyn Jorgensen
702pp. Ref. 528-X

Get the most from 1-2-3 Release 2.01 with this step-by-step guide emphasizing advanced features and practical uses. Topics include data sharing, macros, spreadsheet security, expanded memory, and graphics enhancements.

Mastering 1-2-3 Release 3
Carolyn Jorgensen
682pp. Ref. 517-4

For new Release 3 and experienced Release 2 users, "Mastering" starts with a basic spreadsheet, then introduces spreadsheet and database commands, functions, and macros, and then tells how to analyze 3D spreadsheets and make high-impact reports and graphs. Lotus add-ons are discussed and Fast Tracks are included.

Mastering Enable/OA
Christopher Van Buren
Robert Bixby
540pp. Ref 637-5

This is a structured, hands-on guide to integrated business computing, for users who want to achieve productivity in the shortest possible time. Separate in-depth sections cover word processing, spreadsheets, databases, telecommunications, task integration and macros.

Mastering Excel on the IBM PC
Carl Townsend
628pp. Ref. 403-8

A complete Excel handbook with step-by-step tutorials, sample applications and an extensive reference section. Topics include worksheet fundamentals, formulas and windows, graphics, database techniques, special features, macros and more.

Mastering Framework III
Douglas Hergert
Jonathan Kamin
613pp. Ref. 513-1

Thorough, hands-on treatment of the latest Framework release. An outstanding introduction to integrated software applications, with examples for outlining, spreadsheets, word processing, databases, and more; plus an introduction to FRED programming.

Mastering Quattro Pro 2
Gene Weisskopf
575pp, Ref. 792-4

This hands-on guide and reference takes readers from basic spreadsheets to creating three-dimensional graphs, spreadsheet databases, macros and advanced data analysis. Also covers Paradox Access and translating Lotus 1-2-3 2.2 work sheets. A great tutorial for beginning and intermediate users, this book also serves as a reference for users at all levels.

Mastering SuperCalc5
Greg Harvey
Mary Beth Andrasak
500pp. Ref. 624-3

This book offers a complete and unintimidating guided tour through each feature. With step-by-step lessons, readers learn about the full capabilities of spreadsheet, graphics, and data management functions. Multiple spreadsheets, linked spreadsheets, 3D graphics, and macros are also discussed.

**Mastering Symphony
(Fourth Edition)**
Douglas Cobb
857pp. Ref. 494-1
Thoroughly revised to cover all aspects of
the major upgrade of Symphony Version
2, this Fourth Edition of Doug Cobb's
classic is still "the Symphony bible" to this
complex but even more powerful package. All the new features are discussed
and placed in context with prior versions
so that both new and previous users will
benefit from Cobb's insights.

**Teach Yourself Lotus 1-2-3
Release 2.2**
Jeff Woodward
250pp. Ref. 641-3
Readers match what they see on the
screen with the book's screen-by-screen
action sequences. For new Lotus users,
topics include computer fundamentals,
opening and editing a worksheet, using
graphs, macros, and printing typeset-
quality reports. For Release 2.2.

**Understanding PFS:
First Choice**
Gerry Litton
489pp. Ref. 568-9
From basic commands to complex features, this complete guide to the popular
integrated package is loaded with step-
by-step instructions. Lessons cover creating attractive documents, setting up
easy-to-use databases, working with
spreadsheets and graphics, and
smoothly integrating tasks from different
First Choice modules. For Version 3.0.

ACCOUNTING

**Mastering DacEasy Accounting
(Second Edition)**
Darleen Hartley Yourzek
463pp. Ref. 679-0
This new edition focuses on version 4.0
(with notes on using 3.0), and includes an
introduction to DacEasy Payroll. Packed
with real-world accounting examples, it
covers everything from installing DacEasy
to converting data, setting up applications, processing work and printing custom reports.

HOME MONEY MANAGEMENT

Mastering Quicken 3
Steve Cummings
350pp. Ref. 662-6
With tips on personal financial planning
by Pauline Tai of *Money Magazine*, this
hands-on guide to both Quicken and
Stock! portfolio manager centers on a
variety of valuable examples. Cover
simple check writing, budgeting, tax
accounting, cash flow management, even
payroll.

OPERATING SYSTEMS

The ABC's of DOS 4
Alan R. Miller
275pp. Ref. 583-2
This step-by-step introduction to using
DOS 4 is written especially for beginners.
Filled with simple examples, *The ABC's of
DOS 4* covers the basics of hardware,
software, disks, the system editor EDLIN,
DOS commands, and more.

**ABC's of MS-DOS
(Second Edition)**
Alan R. Miller
233pp. Ref. 493-3
This handy guide to MS-DOS is all many
PC users need to manage their computer
files, organize floppy and hard disks, use
EDLIN, and keep their computers orga-
nized. Additional information is given
about utilities like Sidekick, and there is a
DOS command and program summary.
The second edition is fully updated for
Version 3.3.

**DOS Assembly Language
Programming**
Alan R. Miller
365pp. 487-9
This book covers PC-DOS through 3.3,
and gives clear explanations of how to
assemble, link, and debug 8086, 8088,
80286, and 80386 programs. The
example assembly language routines are
valuable for students and programmers
alike.

DOS Instant Reference
SYBEX Prompter Series
Greg Harvey
Kay Yarborough Nelson
220pp. Ref. 477-1, 4 ¾" × 8"

A complete fingertip reference for fast, easy on-line help:command summaries, syntax, usage and error messages. Organized by function—system commands, file commands, disk management, directories, batch files, I/O, networking, programming, and more. Through Version 3.3.

Encyclopedia DOS
Judd Robbins
1030pp. Ref. 699-5

A comprehensive reference and user's guide to all versions of DOS through 4.0. Offers complete information on every DOS command, with all possible switches and parameters—plus examples of effective usage. An invaluable tool.

Essential OS/2
(Second Edition)
Judd Robbins
445pp. Ref. 609-X

Written by an OS/2 expert, this is the guide to the powerful new resources of the OS/2 operating system standard edition 1.1 with presentation manager. Robbins introduces the standard edition, and details multitasking under OS/2, and the range of commands for installing, starting up, configuring, and running applications. For Version 1.1 Standard Edition.

Essential PC-DOS
(Second Edition)
Myril Clement Shaw
Susan Soltis Shaw
332pp. Ref. 413-5

An authoritative guide to PC-DOS, including version 3.2. Designed to make experts out of beginners, it explores everything from disk management to batch file programming. Includes an 85-page command summary. Through Version 3.2.

Graphics Programming
Under Windows
Brian Myers
Chris Doner
646pp. Ref. 448-8

Straightforward discussion, abundant examples, and a concise reference guide to graphics commands make this book a must for Windows programmers. Topics range from how Windows works to programming for business, animation, CAD, and desktop publishing. For Version 2.

Hard Disk Instant Reference
SYBEX Prompter Series
Judd Robbins
256pp. Ref. 587-5, 4 ¾" × 8"

Compact yet comprehensive, this pocket-sized reference presents the essential information on DOS commands used in managing directories and files, and in optimizing disk configuration. Includes a survey of third-party utility capabilities. Through DOS 4.0.

Inside DOS: A Programmer's Guide
Michael J. Young
490pp. Ref. 710-X

A collection of practical techniques (with source code listings) designed to help you take advantage of the rich resources intrinsic to MS-DOS machines. Designed for the experienced programmer with a basic understanding of C and 8086 assembly language, and DOS fundamentals.

Mastering DOS
(Second Edition)
Judd Robbins
722pp. Ref. 555-7

"The most useful DOS book." This seven-part, in-depth tutorial addresses the needs of users at all levels. Topics range from running applications, to managing files and directories, configuring the system, batch file programming, and techniques for system developers. Through Version 4.

MS-DOS Power User's Guide, Volume I
(Second Edition)
Jonathan Kamin
482pp. Ref. 473-9

A fully revised, expanded edition of our best-selling guide to high-performance DOS techniques and utilities—with details on Version 3.3. Configuration, I/O, directory structures, hard disks, RAM disks, batch file programming, the ANSI.SYS device driver, more. Through Version 3.3.

Understanding DOS 3.3
Judd Robbins
678pp. Ref. 648-0
This best selling, in-depth tutorial addresses the needs of users at all levels with many examples and hands-on exercises. Robbins discusses the fundamentals of DOS, then covers manipulating files and directories, using the DOS editor, printing, communicating, and finishes with a full section on batch files.

Understanding Hard Disk Management on the PC
Jonathan Kamin
500pp. Ref. 561-1
This title is a key productivity tool for all hard disk users who want efficient, error-free file management and organization. Includes details on the best ways to conserve hard disk space when using several memory-guzzling programs. Through DOS 4.

Up & Running with Your Hard Disk
Klaus M Rubsam
140pp. Ref. 666-9
A far-sighted, compact introduction to hard disk installation and basic DOS use. Perfect for PC users who want the practical essentials in the shortest possible time. In 20 basic steps, learn to choose your hard disk, work with accessories, back up data, use DOS utilities to save time, and more.

Up & Running with Windows 286/386
Gabriele Wentges
132pp. Ref. 691-X
This handy 20-step overview gives PC users all the essentials of using Windows—whether for evaluating the software, or getting a fast start. Each self-contained lesson takes just 15 minutes to one hour to complete.

UTILITIES

Mastering the Norton Utilities 5
Peter Dyson
400pp, Ref. 725-8
This complete guide to installing and using the Norton Utilities 5 is a must for beginning and experienced users alike. It offers a clear, detailed description of each utility, with options, uses and examples—

so users can quickly identify the programs they need and put Norton right to work. Includes valuable coverage of the newest Norton enhancements.

Mastering PC Tools Deluxe 6
For Versions 5.5 and 6.0
425pp, Ref. 700-2
An up-to-date guide to the lifesaving utilities in PC Tools Deluxe version 6.0 from installation, to high-speed back-ups, data recovery, file encryption, desktop applications, and more. Includes detailed background on DOS and hardware such as floppies, hard disks, modems and fax cards.

Mastering SideKick Plus
Gene Weisskopf
394pp. Ref. 558-1
Employ all of Sidekick's powerful and expanded features with this hands-on guide to the popular utility. Features include comprehensive and detailed coverage of time management, note taking, outlining, auto dialing, DOS file management, math, and copy-and-paste functions.

Up & Running with Norton Utilities
Rainer Bartel
140pp. Ref. 659-6
Get up and running in the shortest possible time in just 20 lessons or "steps." Learn to restore disks and files, use UnErase, edit your floppy disks, retrieve lost data and more. Or use the book to evaluate the software before you purchase. Through Version 4.2.

Up & Running with PC Tools Deluxe 6
Thomas Holste
180pp. Ref.678-2
Learn to use this software program in just 20 basic steps. Readers get a quick, inexpensive introduction to using the Tools for disaster recovery, disk and file management, and more.

WORD PROCESSING

The ABC's of Microsoft Word (Third Edition)
Alan R. Neibauer
461pp. Ref. 604-9
This is for the novice WORD user who wants to begin producing documents in

the shortest time possible. Each chapter has short, easy-to-follow lessons for both keyboard and mouse, including all the basic editing, formatting and printing functions. Version 5.0.

The ABC's of WordPerfect
Alan R. Neibauer
239pp. Ref. 425-9
This basic introduction to WordPefect consists of short, step-by-step lessons— for new users who want to get going fast. Topics range from simple editing and formatting, to merging, sorting, macros, and more. Includes version 4.2

The ABC's of WordPerfect 5
Alan R. Neibauer
283pp. Ref. 504-2
This introduction explains the basics of desktop publishing with WordPerfect 5: editing, layout, formatting, printing, sorting, merging, and more. Readers are shown how to use WordPerfect 5's new features to produce great-looking reports.

The ABC's of WordPerfect 5.1
Alan R. Neibauer
352pp. Ref. 672-3
Neibauer's delightful writing style makes this clear tutorial an especially effective learning tool. Learn all about 5.1's new drop-down menus and mouse capabilities that reduce the tedious memorization of function keys.

The Complete Guide to MultiMate
Carol Holcomb Dreger
208pp. Ref. 229-9
This step-by-step tutorial is also an excellent reference guide to MultiMate features and uses. Topics include search/replace, library and merge functions, repagination, document defaults and more.

Encyclopedia WordPerfect 5.1
Greg Harvey
Kay Yarborough Nelson
1100pp. Ref. 676-6
This comprehensive, up-to-date Word-Perfect reference is a must for beginning and experienced users alike. With complete, easy-to-find information on every WordPerfect feature and command—and it's organized by practical functions, with business users in mind.

Introduction to WordStar
Arthur Naiman
208pp. Ref. 134-9
This all time bestseller is an engaging first-time introduction to word processing as well as a complete guide to using WordStar—from basic editing to blocks, global searches, formatting, dot commands, SpellStar and MailMerge. Through Version 3.3.

Mastering Microsoft Word on the IBM PC (Fourth Edition)
Matthew Holtz
680pp. Ref. 597-2
This comprehensive, step-by-step guide details all the new desktop publishing developments in this versatile word processor, including details on editing, formatting, printing, and laser printing. Holtz uses sample business documents to demonstrate the use of different fonts, graphics, and complex documents. Includes Fast Track speed notes. For Versions 4 and 5.

Mastering MultiMate Advantage II
Charles Ackerman
407pp. Ref. 482-8
This comprehensive tutorial covers all the capabilities of MultiMate, and highlights the differences between MultiMate Advantage II and previous versions—in pathway support, sorting, math, DOS access, using dBASE III, and more. With many practical examples, and a chapter on the On-File database.

Mastering WordPerfect
Susan Baake Kelly
435pp. Ref. 332-5
Step-by-step training from startup to mastery, featuring practical uses (form letters, newsletters and more), plus advanced topics such as document security and macro creation, sorting and columnar math. Through Version 4.2.

Mastering WordPerfect 5
Susan Baake Kelly
709pp. Ref. 500-X
The revised and expanded version of this definitive guide is now on WordPerfect 5 and covers wordprocessing and basic desktop publishing. As more than 200,000 readers of the original edition can attest, no tutorial approaches it for clarity and depth of treatment. Sorting, line drawing, and laser printing included.

Mastering WordPerfect 5.1
Alan Simpson
1050pp. Ref. 670-7
The ultimate guide for the WordPerfect user. Alan Simpson, the "master communicator," puts you in charge of the latest features of 5.1: new dropdown menus and mouse capabilities, along with the desktop publishing, macro programming, and file conversion functions that have made WordPerfect the most popular word processing program on the market.

Mastering WordStar Release 5.5
Greg Harvey
David J. Clark
450pp. Ref. 491-7
This book is the ultimate reference book for the newest version of WordStar. Readers may use Mastering to look up any word processing function, including the new Version 5 and 5.5 features and enhancements, and find detailed instructions for fundamental to advanced operations.

Microsoft Word Instant Reference for the IBM PC
Matthew Holtz
266pp. Ref. 692-8
Turn here for fast, easy access to concise information on every command and feature of Microsoft Word version 5.0—for editing, formatting, merging, style sheets, macros, and more. With exact keystroke sequences, discussion of command options, and commonly-performed tasks.

Practical WordStar Uses
Julie Anne Arca
303pp. Ref. 107-1
A hands-on guide to WordStar and MailMerge applications, with solutions to comon problems and "recipes" for day-to-day tasks. Formatting, merge-printing and much more; plus a quick-reference command chart and notes on CP/M and PC-DOS. For Version 3.3.

Understanding Professional Write
Gerry Litton
400pp. Ref. 656-1
A complete guide to Professional Write that takes you from creating your first simple document, into a detailed description of all major aspects of the software. Special features place an emphasis on the use of different typestyles to create attractive documents as well as potential problems and suggestions on how to get around them.

WordPerfect 5 Desktop Companion
SYBEX Ready Reference Series
Greg Harvey
Kay Yarborough Nelson
1006pp. Ref. 522-0
Desktop publishing features have been added to this compact encyclopedia. This title offers more detailed, cross-referenced entries on every software feature including page formatting and layout, laser printing and word processing macros. New users of WordPerfect, and those new to Version 5 and desktop publishing will find this easy to use for on-the-job help.

WordPerfect 5 Instant Reference
SYBEX Prompter Series
Greg Harvey
Kay Yarborough Nelson
316pp. Ref. 535-2, 4 ¾" × 8"
This pocket-sized reference has all the program commands for the powerful WordPerfect 5 organized alphabetically for quick access. Each command entry has the exact key sequence, any reveal codes, a list of available options, and option-by-option discussions.

Understanding WordStar 2000
David Kolodney
Thomas Blackadar
275pp. Ref. 554-9
This engaging, fast-paced series of tutorials covers everything from moving the cursor to print enhancements, format files, key glossaries, windows and MailMerge. With practical examples, and notes for former WordStar users.

Visual Guide to WordPerfect
Jeff Woodward
457pp. Ref. 591-3
This is a visual hands-on guide which is ideal for brand new users as the book shows each activity keystroke-by-keystroke. Clear illustrations of computer screen menus are included at every stage. Covers basic editing, formatting lines, paragraphs, and pages, using the block feature, footnotes, search and replace, and more. Through Version 5.

WordPerfect 5.1 Instant Reference
Greg Harvey
Kay Yarborough Nelson
252pp. Ref. 674-X

Instant access to all features and commands of WordPerfect 5.0 and 5.1, highlighting the newest software features. Complete, alphabetical entries provide exact key sequences, codes and options, and step-by-step instructions for many important tasks.

WordPerfect 5.1 Macro Handbook
Kay Yarborough Nelson
532pp, Ref. 687-1

Help yourself to over 150 ready-made macros for WordPerfect versions 5.0 and 5.1. This complete tutorial guide to creating and using work-saving macros is a must for every serious WordPerfect user. Hands-on lessons show you exactly how to record and use your first simple macros—then build to sophisticated skills.

WordPerfect 5.1 Tips and Tricks (Fourth Edition)
Alan R. Neibauer
675pp. Ref. 681-2

This new edition is a real timesaver. For on-the-job guidance and creative new uses, this title covers all versions of WordPerfect up to and including 5.1—streamlining documents, automating with macros, new print enhancements, and more.

WordStar Instant Reference
SYBEX Prompter Series
David J. Clark
314pp. Ref. 543-3, 4 ¾" × 8"

This quick reference provides reminders on the use of the editing, formatting, mailmerge, and document processing commands available through WordStar 4 and 5. Operations are organized alphabetically for easy access. The text includes a survey of the menu system and instructions for installing and customizing WordStar.

DATABASES

The ABC's of dBASE III PLUS
Robert Cowart
264pp. Ref. 379-1

The most efficient way to get beginners up and running with dBASE. Every 'how' and 'why' of database management is demonstrated through tutorials and practical dBASE III PLUS applications.

The ABC's of dBASE IV 1.1
Robert Cowart
350pp, Ref. 632-4

The latest version of dBASE IV is featured in this hands-on introduction. It assumes no previous experience with computers or database management, and uses easy-to-follow lessons to introduce the concepts, build basic skills, and set up some practical applications. Includes report writing and Query by Example.

The ABC's of Paradox 3.5 (Second Edition)
Charles Siegel
334pp, Ref. 785-1

This easy-to-follow, hands-on tutorial is a must for beginning users of Paradox 3.0 and 3.5. Even if you've never used a computer before, you'll be doing useful work in just a few short lessons. A clear introduction to database management and valuable business examples make this a "right-to-work" guide for the practical-minded.

Advanced Techniques in dBASE III PLUS
Alan Simpson
454pp. Ref. 369-4

A full course in database design and structured programming, with routines for inventory control, accounts receivable, system management, and integrated databases.

dBASE Instant Reference
SYBEX Prompter Series
Alan Simpson
471pp. Ref. 484-4; 4 ¾" × 8"

Comprehensive information at a glance: a brief explanation of syntax and usage for every dBASE command, with step-by-step instructions and exact keystroke sequences. Commands are grouped by function in twenty precise categories.

dBASE III PLUS Programmer's Reference Guide
SYBEX Ready Reference Series
Alan Simpson
1056pp. Ref. 508-5

Programmers will save untold hours and effort using this comprehensive, well-organized dBASE encyclopedia. Complete technical details on commands and functions, plus scores of often-needed algorithms.

dBASE IV 1.1 Programmer's Instant Reference (Second Edition)
Alan Simpson
555pp. Ref. 764-9

Enjoy fast, easy access to information often hidden in cumbersome documentation. This handy pocket-sized reference presents information on each command and function in the dBASE IV programming language. Commands are grouped according to their purpose, so readers can locate the correct command for any task—quickly and easily.

dBASE IV User's Instant Reference (Second Edition)
Alan Simpson
356pp. Ref. 786-X

Completely revised to cover the new 1.1 version of dBASE IV, this handy reference guide presents information on every dBASE operation a user can perform. Exact keystroke sequences are presented, and complex tasks are explained step-by-step. It's a great way for newer users to look up the basics, while more experienced users will find it a fast way to locate information on specialized tasks.

Mastering dBASE lil PLUS: A Structured Approach
Carl Townsend
342pp. Ref. 372-4

In-depth treatment of structured programming for custom dBASE solutions. An ideal study and reference guide for applications developers, new and experienced users with an interest in efficient programming.

Mastering dBASE IV Programming
Carl Townsend
496pp. Ref. 540-9

This task-oriented book introduces structured dBASE IV programming and commands by setting up a general ledger system, an invoice system, and a quotation management system. The author carefully explores the unique character of dBASE IV based on his in-depth understanding of the program.

Mastering FoxPro
Charles Seigel
639pp. Ref. 671-5

This guide to the powerful FoxPro DBMS offers a tutorial on database basics, then enables the reader to master new skills and features as needed—with many examples from business. An in-depth tutorial guides users through the development of a complete mailing list system.

Mastering Paradox 3.5
Alan Simpson
650pp. Ref. 677-4

This indispensable, in-depth guide has again been updated for the latest Paradox release, offering the same comprehensive, hands-on treatment featured in highly praised previous editions. It covers everything from database basics to PAL programming—including complex queries and reports, and multi-table applications.

Mastering Q & A (Second Edition)
Greg Harvey
540pp. Ref. 452-6

This hands-on tutorial explores the Q & A Write, File, and Report modules, and the Intelligent Assistant. English-language command processor, macro creation, interfacing with other software, and more, using practical business examples.

Power User's Guide to R:BASE
Alan Simpson
Cheryl Currid
Craig Gillett
446pp. Ref. 354-6

Supercharge your R:BASE applications with this straightforward tutorial that covers system design, structured programming, managing multiple data tables, and more. Sample applications include ready-to-run mailing, inventory and accounts receivable systems. Through Version 2.11.

Understanding dBASE III
Alan Simpson
300pp. Ref. 267-1

dBASE commands and concepts are illustrated throughout with practical, business oriented examples—for mailing list handling, accounts receivable, and inventory design. Contains scores of tips and techniques for maximizing efficiency and meeting special needs.